Optimizing Visual Studio Code for Python Development

Developing More Efficient
and Effective Programs
in Python

Sufyan bin Uzayr

Apress®

Optimizing Visual Studio Code for Python Development: Developing More Efficient and Effective Programs in Python

Sufyan bin Uzayr
Barabanki, India

ISBN-13 (pbk): 978-1-4842-7343-2   ISBN-13 (electronic): 978-1-4842-7344-9
https://doi.org/10.1007/978-1-4842-7344-9

Managing Director, Apress Media LLC: Welmoed Spahr
Acquisitions Editor: Smriti Srivastava
Development Editor: James Markham
Coordinating Editor: Shrikant Vishwakarma

Cover designed by eStudioCalamar

Cover image designed by Pexels

Distributed to the book trade worldwide by Springer Science+Business Media LLC, 1 New York Plaza, Suite 4600, New York, NY 10004. Phone 1-800-SPRINGER, fax (201) 348-4505, e-mail orders-ny@springer-sbm.com, or visit www.springeronline.com. Apress Media, LLC is a California LLC and the sole member (owner) is Springer Science + Business Media Finance Inc (SSBM Finance Inc). SSBM Finance Inc is a **Delaware** corporation.

For information on translations, please e-mail booktranslations@springernature.com; for reprint, paperback, or audio rights, please e-mail bookpermissions@springernature.com, or visit http://www.apress.com/rights-permissions.

Apress titles may be purchased in bulk for academic, corporate, or promotional use. eBook versions and licenses are also available for most titles. For more information, reference our Print and eBook Bulk Sales web page at http://www.apress.com/bulk-sales.

Any source code or other supplementary material referenced by the author in this book is available to readers on GitHub via the book's product page, located at www.apress.com/978-1-4842-7343-2. For more detailed information, please visit http://www.apress.com/source-code.

Printed on acid-free paper

For Mom

Table of Contents

About the Author

Sufyan bin Uzayr is a writer, coder, and entrepreneur with over a decade of experience in the industry. He has authored several books in the past on a diverse range of topics, ranging from history to computers and information technology.

Sufyan is the director of Parakozm, a multinational IT company specializing in EdTech solutions. He also runs Zeba Academy, an online learning and teaching vertical with a focus on STEM fields. He specializes in a wide variety of technologies, such as JavaScript, Dart, WordPress, Drupal, Linux, and Python. He holds multiple degrees, in fields including management, information technology, literature, and political science.

Sufyan is a digital nomad, dividing his time between four countries. He has lived and taught in universities and educational institutions around the globe. Sufyan takes a keen interest in technology, politics, literature, history, and sports, and in his spare time, he enjoys teaching coding and English to young students.

Learn more at sufyanism.com.

About the Technical Reviewer

Mathew Rooney is a coder with 8 years of experience in the web development field. He works with PHP, JavaScript, Python, and offers custom-coded WordPress themes and plugins. Mathew is a firm believer in open-source software and has finished Bachelor of Technology in computer science.

Acknowledgments

There are many people who deserve to be on this page, for this book would not have come into existence without their support. That said, some names deserve a special mention, and I am genuinely grateful to:

- My mother and father, for everything they have done for me.

- Faisal Fareed and Sadaf Fareed, my siblings, for helping with things back home.

- Sana Akhtar Usmani, for all her help and support.

- The Parakozm team, especially Madina Karybzhanova, for offering great amounts of help and assistance during the book-writing process.

- The Apress team, especially Smriti Srivastava, Shrikant Vishwakarma, and James Markham, for ensuring that the book's content, layout, formatting, and everything else remains perfect throughout.

- Reviewers of this book, for going through the manuscript and providing their insight and feedback.

- Typesetters, cover designers, printers, and everyone else, for their part in the development of this book.

ACKNOWLEDGMENTS

- All the folks associated with Zeba Academy, either directly or indirectly, for their help and support.

- The Python and VS Code community at large, for all their hard work and efforts.

—Sufyan bin Uzayr

Introduction

Visual Studio Code (VS Code) is a great open-source code editor created by Microsoft for Windows, Linux, and macOS. Widely applied, standard features include support for debugging, syntax highlighting, automatic code completion, snippets, code restructuring, and embedded Git. Developers from all over the world are free to edit the design theme, keyboard shortcuts, and preferences, as well as install essential and extra extensions to upgrade the general project versatility.

Chapters at a Glance

Chapter 1, "Introduction to Visual Studio Code," reviews how to set up VS Code as well as provide an overview of the basic features, such as:

- **User interface:** Provides the view of the documentation for VS Code.

- **Setup overview:** Analyzes documentation for starting up and running with VS Code, including platform-related setup.

- **Keyboard shortcuts:** Provides customization options for your own shortcuts and installation of Keymap extensions.

- **Keybinding extensions:** Covers how to install a Keymap extension and how to bring the keybindings from other editors to VS Code.

Chapter 2, "Getting Started with Python Programs in Visual Studio Code," explains in detail how to set up your VS Code for Python Development. For the sake of demonstrating with examples, you'll see how to install most of the tools on Windows.

Chapter 3, "Setting Up the Environment and Testing," demonstrates how to install the top 8 Python extensions by typing Python in the Extensions item on the Activity Bar.

Chapter 4, "Working with Python Frameworks," discusses using Python frameworks, such as Django and Flask. We will discuss topics such as Python web development, Django apps, Flask development, and so on.

Chapter 5, "Working with Containers and MS Azure," covers Python development in VS Code in assonance with MS Azure. Azure services can be used for speedy deployment and building of production level apps. With VS Code, Azure offers neat integration and this chapter discusses the same.

CHAPTER 1

Introduction to Visual Studio Code

Visual Studio Code (VS Code) is an open-source code editor created by Microsoft for Windows, Linux, and macOS (Figure 1-1). Widely popular standard features include support for debugging, syntax highlighting, automatic code completion, snippets, code restructuring, and embedded Git. Users are free to change the design theme, keyboard shortcuts, and preferences, as well as install additional extensions to upgrade the overall project functionality.

Microsoft first introduced VS Code at the 2015 Build conference. By 2019 VS Code ranked as the most popular developer environment tool, with 50.7% of 87,317 respondents reporting that they regularly apply it.

© Sufyan bin Uzayr 2021
S. bin Uzayr, *Optimizing Visual Studio Code for Python Development*,
https://doi.org/10.1007/978-1-4842-7344-9_1

Figure 1-1. *Visual Studio Code, a free and open-source code editor*

In this chapter, we will walk you through setting up VS Code as well as provide an overview of the basic features:

- **User interface:** viewing the documentation for VS Code.

- **Setup overview:** documentation for starting up and running with VS Code, including platform-related setup.

- **Keyboard shortcuts:** customization options for your own shortcuts and installation of Keymap extensions.

- **Keybinding extensions:** how to install a Keymap extension to bring the keybindings from your previous editor to VS Code.

User Interface

According to the original intent, VS Code is a code editor. Similar to many other code editors, VS Code has a common user interface and layout of an explorer on the left, displaying all of the files and folders you have access to, and an editor on the right, presenting the content of the files you have opened.

Basic Layout

VS Code comes with a straightforward yet intuitive layout that utilizes all the space provided for the editor, while leaving some room to browse and access the full context of your folder or the ongoing project. The User Interface is divided into five main areas:

- **Editor:** The main space for you to edit current files. You can open as many editors as you need side by side, as well as vertically and horizontally.

- **SideBar:** This area has different views such as the Explorer, to provide a maximum assistance while you are working on your project.

- **Status Bar:** Information about the current project and the files you are editing.

- **Activity Bar:** Placed on the far left-hand side, this area enables you to switch between views and gives you additional context-specific measures—for instance, the number of outgoing changes.

- **Panels:** You can show different panels below the editor area for output or debug content, errors, and warnings, or integrated information. The panel can also be shifted to the right for more vertical space.

Each time you launch VS Code, it opens up in the same state it was in when you last left it. The folder, layout, and opened files will be preserved the same. Open files in each editor are displayed with tabbed headers (Tabs) at the top of the editor region. To learn more information about tabbed headers, see the details of the Tabs section. You can also move the Sidebar to the right-hand side (View ➤ Move Side Bar Right) or enhance its visibility (Ctrl+B).

Side-By-Side Editing

As previously mentioned, you can open as many editors as you like side-by-side vertically as well as horizontally. If you already have one editor open, there are various ways of placing another editor to the side of the existing one:

- Alt-click on a file in the Explorer.

- Ctrl+\ to split the active editor into two.

- Open to the Side (Ctrl+Enter) from the Explorer context menu on a file.

- Click the Split Editor button in the upper right of an editor.

- Drag and drop a file to any side of the editor region.

- Ctrl+Enter (macOS: Cmd+Enter) in the Quick Open (Ctrl+P) file list.

Once you open another file, the editor that is in progress will display the content of that file. So if you have two editors side by side and you need to open file doc.cs into the right-hand editor, make sure that editor is active (by clicking on it) before opening file doc.cs.

By default, editors are made to open on the right-hand side of the active one. You can change this pattern through the setting workbench. editor.openSideBySideDirection and modify to open new editors to the bottom of the active one instead. At the same time, when you have more than one editor active, you can switch between them easily by holding the Ctrl (macOS: Cmd) key and pressing 1, 2, and 3. In addition, you can resize editors and reorder them if you would like to: simply drag and drop the editor title area to reposition or resize the editor.

Minimap

A Minimap (code outline) allows you to get a high-level overview of your source code, which is quite useful for easy navigation and code comprehension. A file's minimap is displayed on the right side of the editor. You can also click or drag the shaded area to quickly switch to different sections of your file. It is also worth noting that you can move the minimap to the left-hand side or even disable it completely by simply setting "editor.minimap.side":, "left", or "editor.minimap.enabled": false in your user or workspace settings.

Indent Guides

The image above the editor also shows vertical lines or indentation guides that are there to help you freely observe matching indent levels. If you would like to turn off those indent guides, you should set "editor.renderIndentGuides": false in your user or workspace settings.

Breadcrumbs

If you take a look at the editor once again, you will notice it has a navigation bar above its contents that is named Breadcrumbs. It is there to show your current location and let you quickly navigate between folders, files, and symbols.

Breadcrumbs also tend to display the file path, and if the active file type has language support for symbols, it displays the symbol path up to the cursor position. You can switch off Breadcrumbs with the View ➤ Show Breadcrumbs simple command. You can also access the same information about the Breadcrumbs feature at the Breadcrumbs section of the editor.

Explorer

The Explorer is a tool used to browse, open, and operate all of the files and folders in your editing project. Since VS Code is file- and folder-based, you can get started at any time simply by opening a file or folder in VS Code. Once you open a folder in VS Code, the contents of the folder are shown in the Explorer. You can do many modifications from here, such as:

- Create, delete, and rename files and folders.

- Change the location of files and folders by using drag and drop.

- See the context menu to see all options.

Moreover, you can drag and drop files into the Explorer from outside VS Code to make a VS copy of them, so that if the explorer is empty, VS Code will access them instead.

VS Code also works very well with other tools that you might use, especially command-line tools. If you need to run a command-line tool in the context of the folder you have open in VS Code, right-click the folder and select Open in Command Prompt (or Open in Terminal on macOS or Linux).

At the same time, you can navigate to the location of a file or folder in the native Explorer by right-clicking on a file or folder and selecting Reveal in Explorer (or Reveal in Finder on macOS, or Open Containing Folder on Linux). You may also type Ctrl+P (Quick Open option) to quickly search and open a file by its name.

By default, VS Code does not open some folders from the Explorer (for example, .git). In this case, you can use the files.exclude setting to edit rules for hiding files and folders from the Explorer. However, if you have any derived resource files, such as *.meta in Unity or *.js in a TypeScript project, then this solution is not really going to be useful. Please note that for Unity to exclude the *.cs.metafiles, the pattern to select would be "**/*. cs.meta": true. For TypeScript, you can exclude generated JavaScript for TypeScript files with "**/*.js": {"when": "$(basename).ts"}.

Multiselection

You can choose multiple files in the File Explorer and OPEN EDITORS view to complete actions (Delete, Drag and Drop, Open to the Side) on multiple items. Simply use the Ctrl/Cmd key with a click to select individual files and Shift + click to select a range. If you select two items, you can now use the context menu Compare Selected command to quickly differentiate the two files. Also, remember that in earlier VS Code releases, clicking with the Ctrl/Cmd key pressed would open a file in a new Editor Group to the side. If you would still like this feature, you can use the workbench.list. multiSelectModifier setting to modify multiselection to use the Alt key by "workbench.list.multiSelectModifier": "alt".

Filtering the Document Tree

It is possible to filter the currently visible files in the File Explorer. You can simply start typing part of the file name you want to match, keeping the focus on the File Explorer. You will be able to see a filter box in the top-right of the File Explorer presenting what you have typed so far, and matching file names will be highlighted. Once you press the cursor keys to move up and down the file list, it will switch between matching files or folders. However, switching over the filter box and selecting Enable Filter on Type will show only matching files and folders. You can apply the X Clear button to clear the filter.

Outline View

The Outline view is a section at the bottom of the File Explorer. When activated, it will show the symbol tree of the currently active editor. The Outline view has different Sort By modes and optional cursor tracking, and supports the usual open gestures. It also has an input box that can search for filters and symbols as you type. Errors and warnings are also displayed in the Outline view, allowing you to see a glimpse of a problem as well as its location.

As for symbols, the view relies heavily on the data computed by your installed extensions for different file types. For instance, the built-in Markdown support returns the Markdown header hierarchy for a Markdown file's symbols.

Markdown Outline View

There are a few Outline view settings that allow you to enable and disable items and operate with errors and warnings display (all enabled by default):[1]

- **outline.icons:** toggle rendering outline elements with icons.

- **outline.problems.enabled:** shows errors and warnings on outline elements.

- **outline.problems.badges:** toggle using badges for errors and warnings.

- **outline.problems.colors:** toggle using colors for errors and warnings.

Open Editors

At the top of the Explorer, there is a section labeled as OPEN EDITORS that displays a list of active files or previews. There might also be some files visible that you previously opened in VS Code. For example, a file will be listed in the OPEN EDITORS view if you make a change to a file, double-click a file's header, double-click a file in the Explorer, or open a file that is not part of the current folder. By clicking an item in the OPEN EDITORS view, it becomes active in VS Code. Once you are finished with your project and wish to remove files individually from the OPEN EDITORS view, or remove all files, you can do so by using the View: Close All Editors or View and then Close All Editors in Group actions.

---

[1] Visual Studio Code, "Markdown and Visual Studio Code," https://code.visualstudio.com/docs/languages/markdown, accessed July 29, 2021.

Views

The File Explorer is just one of the Views available in VS Code. There are also Views for:[2]

- **Search:** Provides global search and replace across your open folder.

- **Source Control:** VS Code includes Git source control by default.

- **Run:** VS Code's Run and Debug View displays variables, call stacks, and breakpoints.

- **Extensions:** Installs and manages your extensions within VS Code.

- **Custom views:** Views contributed by extensions.

Any of these views can be accessed by using the View: Open View command.

Activity Bar

The Activity Bar on your left is designed for you to easily switch between Views. You can also reorder Views by dragging and dropping them on the Activity Bar, or stow away a View entirely with the right-click Hide from Activity Bar.

Command Palette

VS Code is also easily accessible from the keyboard. The most useful key combination to know is Ctrl+Shift+P, which calls for the Command Palette. With the Command Palette you have access to all of the functionality of VS

---

[2] Visual Studio Code, "User and Workspace Settings," https://code.visualstudio.com/docs/getstarted/settings, accessed July 29, 2021.

Code, including keyboard shortcuts for the most implemented operations. The Command Palette provides access to many commands. You can manage editor commands, open files, search for items, and see a quick outline of a file, all while using the same interactive window. Following are a few navigation combinations:[3]

- Ctrl+P will let you navigate to any file or symbol by typing its name.

- Ctrl+Tab will cycle you through the last set of files opened.

- Ctrl+Shift+P will bring you directly to the editor commands.

- Ctrl+Shift+O will let you navigate to a specific symbol in a file.

- Ctrl+G will let you navigate to a specific line in a file.

- Type ? into the input field to get a list of available commands you can execute from Quick Open Help.

Configuring the Editor

VS Code has many options for you to configure the editor. From the View menu you can hide or toggle various bits of the user interface, such as the Side Bar, Status Bar, and Activity Bar.

---

[3] Visual Studio Code, "User and Workspace Settings."

Hiding the Menu Bar (for Windows, Linux)

You can hide the Menu Bar on Windows and Linux by selecting the setting window.menuBarVisibility from classic to toggle. The toggle setting means that a single press of the Alt key will show the Menu Bar again.

You can also remove the Menu Bar on Windows and Linux with the View ➤ Toggle Menu Bar command. This command switches window. menuBarVisibility from classic to compact, resulting in the Menu Bar moving into the Activity Bar. To move back to the Menu Bar to the classic position, select the View ➤ Toggle Menu Bar command again.

Settings

Most basic editor configurations are kept in settings that can be modified directly. You can set options globally through user settings, or per project or file through workspace settings. Settings options are kept in a settings. json file. You can follow the path Select File ➤ Preferences ➤ Settings (or press Ctrl+,) to edit the user settings.json file. To change workspace settings, click the WORKSPACE SETTINGS tab to edit the workspace settings.json file. Note that for macOS users, the Preferences menu is located under Code, not File; please follow Code ➤ Preferences ➤ Settings.

You can access the VS Code Default Settings in the left window, and your editable settings.json on the right. It is also possible to easily filter settings in the Default Settings using the search box at the top. You can copy a setting over to the editable settings.json on the right by clicking on the edit icon to the left of the setting. Settings with a fixed set of values let you select a primary value as a section of their edit icon menu. After editing your settings, type Ctrl+S to settle your changes. The changes will take effect instantly. Workspace settings will override User settings and are beneficial for sharing particular project settings.

Zen Mode

Zen mode enables you to focus on your code by removing all User Interface items (Activity Bar, Status Bar, Side Bar, and Panel) except the editor, displaying the full screen and centering the editor layout only. Zen mode can be toggled using the View menu, Command Palette or by the shortcut, Ctrl+K Z. To exit Zen mode, press double Esc. The transition to full screen can be disabled via zenMode.fullScreen. Zen mode can be further modified using the following settings: zenMode.hideStatusBar, zenMode.hideTabs, zenMode.fullScreen, zenMode.restore, and zenMode.centerLayout.

Centered Editor Layout

Centered editor layout lets you center-align the editor area. This is especially useful if you find yourself working with a single editor on a large monitor. You can apply the sashes on the side to resize the view with the Alt key, and using the same method you can also independently move the sashes.

Tabs

VS Code displays open items with tabbed headings or Tabs in the title area above the editor. If you open a file, a new Tab is added for that file. Tabs allow you to quickly navigate between files, and you can drag and drop tabs to reorder them as you wish. When you have more open items than can fit in the title area, you can apply the Show Opened Editors command to show a dropdown list of tabbed items.

If you do not want to use Tabs, you can turn off the feature by setting the workbench.editor.showTabs setting to false: "workbench.editor.showTabs": false.

13

Tab Ordering

By default, new Tabs are included to the right of the existing Tabs, but you can administer where you would like new Tabs to appear with the workbench.editor.openPositioning setting. For instance, you might like new tabbed items to appear on the left, by using "workbench.editor .openPositioning": "left".

Preview Mode

Once you single-click or select a file in the Explorer, it is shown in a presentation mode and reuses an existing Tab. This is particularly helpful if you just need to quickly browse files and do not want each file you accessed to have its own Tab. When you start editing the file or use double-click to open the file from the Explorer, a new Tab is assigned to that file. Preview mode is indicated by italics in the Tab heading: *preview mode*.

If you would rather not see the preview mode and always make a new Tab, you can control the pattern with these settings:

- **workbench.editor.enablePreview:** to globally enable or disable preview editors.

- **workbench.editor.enablePreviewFromQuickOpen:** to enable or disable preview editors when opened from Quick Open.

Editor Groups

If you split an editor via the Split Editor or Open to the Side commands, a new editor region that can hold a group of items is created instead. At the same time, you can open as many editor regions as you like side-by-side vertically and horizontally. You can see them in order in the OPEN EDITORS section at the top of the Explorer view. The OPEN EDITORS section also allows you to Drag and Drop editor groups on the workbench, move individual Tabs between groups, and quickly close entire groups by clicking on Close All.

Be sure that VS Code uses editor groups whether or not you have any Tabs on. Without Tabs, editor groups are a stack of your open items with the most recently searched item visible in the editor pane. By default, editor groups are structured in vertical columns when you split an editor to open it to the side. You can also arrange editor groups in any layout you like, both vertically and horizontally.

In order to support flexible layouts, you should create empty editor groups. By default, closing the last editor of an editor group will also close the group itself, but you can modify this behavior with the new setting workbench.editor.closeEmptyGroups: false. You can also see if there are any predefined set of editor layouts in the View ➤ Editor Layout menu.

Editors that open to the side by clicking the editor toolbar Split Editor action will normally open to the right-hand side of the active editor. If you prefer to open editors below the active one, configure the new setting workbench.editor.openSideBySideDirection: down.

There are plenty of keyboard commands for adjusting the editor layout with the keyboard alone, but if you prefer to use the mouse, drag and drop is the fastest method to split the editor into any direction. In addition, if you press and hold the Alt key while switching over the toolbar action to split an editor, it will offer to split to the other orientation. This is another fast way to split either to the right or to the bottom.

Keyboard Shortcuts

It will also be very beneficial for you to know some handy keyboard shortcuts to quickly navigate between editors and editor groups. Some of the most widely used ones are the following:[4]

- Ctrl+PageDown go to the right editor.

- Ctrl+PageUp go to the left editor.

- Ctrl+Tab open the previous editor in the editor group MRU list.

- Ctrl+1 go to the leftmost editor group.

- Ctrl+2 go to the center editor group.

- Ctrl+3 go to the rightmost editor group.

- Ctrl+F4 close the active editor.

- Ctrl+K W close all editors in the editor group.

- Ctrl+K Ctrl+W close all editors.

Disabling Preview Mode

Without Tabs, the OPEN EDITORS section of the File Explorer is a great way to do file navigation. With preview editor mode, files are not shown in the OPEN EDITOR list, nor editor group on single-click open. You can turn this feature off through the workbench.editor.enablePreview and workbench.editor.enablePreviewFromQuickOpen settings.

---

[4]Visual Studio Code, "User Interface," https://code.visualstudio.com/docs/getstarted/userinterface, accessed July 29, 2021.

Using Ctrl+Tab to Navigate in Entire Editor History

You can edit keybindings for Ctrl+Tab to show you a list of all opened editors from the history independent from the active editor group. You can edit your keybindings and add the following by using:

```
{ "key": "ctrl+tab", "command":
"workbench.action.openPreviousEditorFromHistory" },
{ "key": "ctrl+tab", "command":
"workbench.action.quickOpenNavigateNext", "when": "inQuickOpen" }
```

Closing an Entire Group Instead of a Single Editor

If you want to repeat the behavior of VS Code closing an entire group when closing one editor, you can bind the following in your keybindings by using:

```
macOS: { "key": "cmd+w", "command":
"workbench.action.closeEditorsInGroup" }
Windows/Linux: { "key": "ctrl+w", "command":
"workbench.action.closeEditorsInGroup" }
```

Window Management

VS Code has some options to operate to determine how windows can be opened or restored between sessions. The settings window.openFoldersInNewWindow and window.openFilesInNewWindow are used to configure opening new windows or reusing the last active window for files or folders and possible values by default.

If edited to turn to default conditions, VS Code will restore all windows you worked on during your previous session. However, there can still be cases where this setting is ignored (for instance, if using the -new-window or -reuse-window command-line option).

The window.restoreWindows setting tells VS Code how to restore the opened windows of your previous session. You can also change this setting to never reopen any windows and always start with an empty VS Code instance.

We will now take a look at how to set up VS Code for Python development.

Setting Up Visual Studio Code

Getting and activating VS Code is easy and quick. All it takes is a small download and then you can install it in a matter of minutes (Figure 1-2).

Figure 1-2. *Setting up VS Code*

Cross-Platform

VS Code is a free code editor that runs on the macOS, Linux, and Windows operating systems.

For smoother installation you can follow the following platform-specific guides:[5]

MacOS

1. Download VS Code for macOS.

2. Open the browser's download list and locate the downloaded archive.

3. Select the magnifying glass icon to open the archive in Finder.

4. Drag VS Code.app to the Applications folder, making it available in the macOS Launchpad.

5. Add VS Code to your Dock by right-clicking on the icon to bring up the context menu and choosing Options, Keep in Dock.

Linux

VS Code is officially distributed as a Snap package in the Snap Store, and can also be downloaded from the official site as an RPM or DEB package.

You can install it by running: sudo snap install --classic code # or code-insiders.

---

[5]Visual Studio Code, "Setting Up Visual Studio Code," https://code. visualstudio.com/docs/setup/setup-overview, accessed July 29, 2021.

Once installed, the Snap daemon will take care of automatically updating VS Code in the background. You can also expect to get an in-product update notification whenever a new update is available.

Windows

1. Download the VS Code installer for Windows.

2. Once it is downloaded, run the installer (VSCodeUserSetup-{version}.exe). This will only take a minute.

3. By default, VS Code is installed under C:\users\ {username}\AppData\Local\Programs\Microsoft VS Code.

VS Code is lightweight and should run on most available hardware and platform versions. You can review the System Requirements to see whether your computer configuration is supported.

Updating Cadence

VS Code releases a new version every month with new features and progressive bug fixes. Most platforms have auto-updating installed, so you will be prompted to look for the new release when it becomes available. You can also manually check for updates by running Help ➤ Check for Updates on Linux and Windows, or running Code ➤ Check for Updates on macOS. Additionally, you can also disable auto-update if you would like to update VS Code according to your own schedule.

Insiders Nightly Build

If you'd like to check out VS Code nightly builds to get access to new features earlier than the rest of the users or to verify bug fixes, you can install the Insiders build. The Insiders build installs side by side with the monthly Stable build, and you can freely incorporate and work with both on the same machine. The Insiders build is the same tool that the VS Code development team uses on a daily basis. If you have valuable feedback about the new features to offer, the development team would really appreciate it.

Portable Mode

VS Code also supports Portable mode installation. This mode ensures that all data created and maintained by VS Code is stored in close quarters so that when necessary it can be moved around across environments, even on a USB drive.

Additional Components

VS Code is an editor with a relatively small footprint. Unlike other traditional editors that tend to include every other function, with VS Code you can tune and customize your installation to the development technologies most important to you.

Extensions

VS Code extensions let third parties add support for the following:

- **Languages:** C++, C#, Go, Java, Python
- **Tools:** ESLint, JSHint , PowerShell

- **Debuggers:** PHP XDebug

- **Keymaps:** Vim, Sublime Text, IntelliJ, Emacs, Atom, Brackets, Visual Studio, Eclipse

Extensions smoothly integrate into VS Code's User Interface, commands, and task running systems, so you will find it easy to operate with different technologies through VS Code's shared interface.

Key Bindings for Visual Studio Code

VS Code offers you an option to manage most tasks directly from the keyboard (Figure 1-3). This section lists out the default bindings (keyboard shortcuts) and gives you an overview of how you can update them.

Figure 1-3. *Using keyboard shortcuts in VS Code*

Keyboard Shortcuts Editor

VS Code has many simple keyboard shortcuts using Keyboard Shortcuts editor. It illustrates all available commands with and without keybindings, and you can easily change, remove, and update these using the available options. It also has a search box on the top that is useful when searching for commands or keybindings. You can open this editor by looking at the menu under File ➤ Preferences ➤ Keyboard Shortcuts (Code ➤ Preferences ➤ Keyboard Shortcuts on macOS). You can also access a printable version of these keyboard shortcuts at Help ➤ Keyboard Shortcut Reference and get a condensed PDF version suitable for printing as a user-friendly reference.

Detecting Keybinding Conflicts

If you have too many extensions installed or you have customized most of your keyboard shortcuts, you may at times face keybinding conflicts where the same keyboard shortcut is mapped to perform several commands. This can result in confusing occurrences, especially if different keybindings are going in and out of scope when you keep working with the editor. From time to time you should check on the Keyboard Shortcuts editor that has a context menu command Show Same Keybindings, which is used to filter the keybindings based on a keyboard shortcut to display and potentially prevent any conflicts.

Troubleshooting Keybindings

To troubleshoot keybindings problems, you can activate the command Developer: Toggle Keyboard Shortcuts Troubleshooting. This will help to perform logging of dispatched keyboard shortcuts and will give access to the output panel with the corresponding log file.

With it, you can later press your desired keybinding and check what keyboard shortcut VS Code uses and what command is activated.

Keyboard Rules

Each rule consists of the following:[6]

- a key that defines the pressed keys.

- a command containing the identifier of the command to execute.

- an optional when clause containing a Boolean expression that will be calculated depending on the current context.

Two separate keypress actions known as Chords are described by separating the two keypresses with space. For example, Ctrl+K Ctrl+C.

When a key is pressed:

- the rules are assessed from bottom to top.

- the first rule that matches, both the key and in terms of when is accepted.

- no more rules are processed.

- if a rule is found and has a command set too, the command is implemented.

The additional keybindings.json rules are omitted at runtime to the bottom of the default rules, therefore allowing them to overwrite the default rules. The keybindings.json file is observed by VS Code, so editing it while VS Code is running will upgrade the rules at runtime.

The keyboard shortcuts dispatching is completed by analyzing a list of rules that are stored in JSON. To illustrate with a few examples:[7]

---

[6] Visual Studio Code, "Key Bindings for Visual Studio Code," https://code.visualstudio.com/docs/getstarted/keybindings, accessed July 29, 2021.

[7] Visual Studio Code, "Key Bindings for Visual Studio Code."

```
// Keybindings that are active when the focus is in the editor:
{ "key": "home",              "command": "cursorHome",
              "when": "editorTextFocus" },
{ "key": "shift+home",        "command": "cursorHomeSelect"
,             "when": "editorTextFocus" },

// Keybindings that are complementary:
{ "key": "f5",                "command":
"workbench.action.debug.continue", "when": "inDebugMode" },
{ "key": "f5",                "command":
"workbench.action.debug.start",     "when": "!inDebugMode" },

// Global keybindings:
{ "key": "ctrl+f",            "command": "actions.find" },
{ "key": "alt+left",          "command":
"workbench.action.navigateBack" },
{ "key": "alt+right",         "command":
"workbench.action.navigateForward" },

// Global keybindings using chords (two separate keypress actions):
{ "key": "ctrl+k enter",      "command":
"workbench.action.keepEditor" },
{ "key": "ctrl+k ctrl+w",     "command":
"workbench.action.closeAllEditors" },
```

Accepted Keys

The key is made up of modifiers and the key itself. The following modifiers are accepted:

Platform	Modifiers
macOS	Ctrl+, Shift+, Alt+, Cmd+
Windows	Ctrl+, Shift+, Alt+, Win+
Linux	Ctrl+, Shift+, Alt+, Meta+

The following keys are accepted:

- f1-f19, a-z, 0-9

- `` ` ``, -, =, [,], \, ;, ', ,, ., /

- left, up, right, down, pageup, pagedown, end, home

- tab, enter, escape, space, backspace, delete

- pausebreak, capslock, insert

- numpad0-numpad9, numpad_multiply, numpad_add, numpad_separator

- numpad_subtract, numpad_decimal, numpad_divide

Command Arguments

You can call on command with arguments. This is especially helpful if you usually perform the same operation on a specific file or folder. You can include a custom keyboard shortcut to do exactly what you need it to do. The following is an example of overriding the Enter key to print some text:

```
{
  "key": "enter",
  "command": "type",
  "args": { "text": "Hello There" },
  "when": "editorTextFocus"
}
```

The type command will receive {"text": "Hello There"} as its first argument and add "Hello There" to the file instead of producing the default command.

Removing a Specific Key Binding Rule

You can script a key binding rule that targets the dismissal of a specific default key binding. With keybindings.json it was always acceptable to redefine all the key bindings of VS Code, but it can be challenging to make a small addition, especially around overloaded keys, such as Tab or Escape. In order to hide a specific key binding, add a - to the command and the rule will be a removal one.

Keyboard Layout-Independent Nindings

Using scan codes, it is manageable to define keybindings that do not change with the modification of the keyboard layout. For example: { "key": "cmd+[Slash]", "command": "editor.action.commentLine", and "when": "editorTextFocus" }.

The following scan codes are accepted:

```
[F1]-[F19], [KeyA]-[KeyZ], [Digit0]-[Digit9]
[Backquote], [Minus], [Equal], [BracketLeft], [BracketRight],
[Backslash], [Semicolon], [Quote], [Comma], [Period], [Slash]
[ArrowLeft], [ArrowUp], [ArrowRight], [ArrowDown], [PageUp],
[PageDown], [End], [Home]
[Tab], [Enter], [Escape], [Space], [Backspace], [Delete]
[Pause], [CapsLock], [Insert]
[Numpad0]-[Numpad9], [NumpadMultiply], [NumpadAdd],
[NumpadComma]
[NumpadSubtract], [NumpadDecimal], [NumpadDivide]
```

When Clause Contexts

VS Code gives you full control over when your key bindings are activated through the optional when clause. If some key bindings do not have a when clause, those key binding are globally available at all times. A when clause relates to either Boolean true or false for operating key bindings.

In addition, VS Code sets various context keys and specific values depending on what elements are available and active in the VS Code User Interface. For instance, the built-in Start Debugging command has the keyboard shortcut F5, which is only enabled when there is an appropriate debugger available (context debuggersAvailable is true) and the editor is not in debug mode (context inDebugMode is false).

Conditional Operators

For when clause conditional expressions, the conditional operators in Table 1-1 are used for keybindings.[8]

Table 1-1. *Conditional operators*

Operator	Symbol	Example
Equality	==	"editorLangId == typescript"
Inequality	!=	"resourceExtname != .js"
Or	||	"isLinux||isWindows"
And	&&	"textInputFocus && !editorReadonly"
Matches	=~	"resourceScheme =~ /^untitled$\|^file$/"

---

[8] Visual Studio Code, "Key Bindings for Visual Studio Code."

Available Contexts

You can see some of the available contexts at hand when clause contexts in the when clause context reference. The list there is not as exhaustive, and you can look for other when clause contexts by searching and filtering in the Keyboard Shortcuts editor (Preferences: Open Keyboard Shortcuts) or reviewing the Default Keybindings JSON file (Preferences: Open Default Keyboard Shortcuts (JSON)). Tables 1-2 through 1-12 provides shortcuts for some basic commands.[9]

Table 1-2. *Basic editing*

Command	Key	Command id
Cut line (empty selection)	Ctrl+X	editor.action.clipboardCutAction
Copy line (empty selection)	Ctrl+C	editor.action.clipboardCopyAction
Paste	Ctrl+V	editor.action.clipboardPasteAction
Delete Line	Ctrl+Shift+K	editor.action.deleteLines
Insert Line Below	Ctrl+Enter	editor.action.insertLineAfter
Insert Line Above	Ctrl+Shift+Enter	editor.action.insertLineBefore
Move Line Down	Alt+Down	editor.action.moveLinesDownAction
Move Line Up	Alt+Up	editor.action.moveLinesUpAction
Copy Line Down	Shift+Alt+Down	editor.action.copyLinesDownAction
Copy Line Up	Shift+Alt+Up	editor.action.copyLinesUpAction

(*continued*)

---

[9] Visual Studio Code, "When Clause Contexts," https://code.visualstudio.com/api/references/when-clause-contexts, VS Code, web, accessed July 29, 2021.

Table 1-2. (*continued*)

Command	Key	Command id
Undo	Ctrl+Z	undo
Redo	Ctrl+Y	redo
Add Selection To Next Find Match	Ctrl+D	editor.action .addSelectionToNextFindMatch
Move Last Selection To Next Find Match	Ctrl+K	editor.action .moveSelectionToNextFindMatch
Undo last cursor operation	Ctrl+U	cursorUndo
Insert cursor at end of line	Shift+Alt+I	editor.action .insertCursorAtEndOfEachLineSelected
Select all occurrences of current selection	Ctrl+Shift+L	editor.action.selectHighlights
Select all occurrences of current word	Ctrl+F2	editor.action.changeAll
Select current line	Ctrl+L	expandLineSelection
Insert Cursor Below	Ctrl+Alt+Down	editor.action.insertCursorBelow
Insert Cursor Above	Ctrl+Alt+Up	editor.action.insertCursorAbove
Jump to matching bracket	Ctrl+Shift+\	editor.action.jumpToBracket
Indent Line	Ctrl+]	editor.action.indentLines
Outdent Line	Ctrl+[	editor.action.outdentLines
Go to Beginning of Line	Home	cursorHome

(*continued*)

Table 1-2. (*continued*)

Command	Key	Command id
Go to End of Line	End	cursorEnd
Go to End of File	Ctrl+End	cursorBottom
Go to Beginning of File	Ctrl+Home	cursorTop
Scroll Line Down	Ctrl+Down	scrollLineDown
Scroll Line Up	Ctrl+Up	scrollLineUp
Scroll Page Down	Alt+PageDown	scrollPageDown
Scroll Page Up	Alt+PageUp	scrollPageUp
Fold (collapse) region	Ctrl+Shift+[	editor.fold
Unfold (uncollapse) region	Ctrl+Shift+]	editor.unfold
Fold (collapse) all subregions	Ctrl+K Ctrl+[	editor.foldRecursively
Unfold (uncollapse) all subregions	Ctrl+K Ctrl+]	editor.unfoldRecursively
Fold (collapse) all regions	Ctrl+K Ctrl+0	editor.foldAll
Unfold (uncollapse) all regions	Ctrl+K Ctrl+J	editor.unfoldAll
Add Line Comment	Ctrl+K Ctrl+C	editor.action.addCommentLine
Remove Line Comment	Ctrl+K Ctrl+U	editor.action.removeCommentLine
Toggle Line Comment	Ctrl+/	editor.action.commentLine

(*continued*)

Table 1-2. (*continued*)

Command	Key	Command id
Toggle Block Comment	Shift+Alt+A	editor.action.blockComment
Find	Ctrl+F	actions.find
Replace	Ctrl+H	editor.action.startFindReplaceAction
Find Next	Enter	editor.action.nextMatchFindAction
Find Previous	Shift+Enter	editor.action.previousMatchFindAction
Select All Occurrences of Find Match	Alt+Enter	editor.action.selectAllMatches
Toggle Find Case Sensitive	Alt+C	toggleFindCaseSensitive
Toggle Find Regex	Alt+R	toggleFindRegex
Toggle Find Whole Word	Alt+W	toggleFindWholeWord
Toggle Use of Tab Key for Setting Focus	Ctrl+M	editor.action.toggleTabFocusMode
Toggle Render Whitespace	unassigned	toggleRenderWhitespace
Toggle Word Wrap	Alt+Z	editor.action.toggleWordWrap

Table 1-3. *Rich languages editing*

Command	Key	Command id
Trigger Suggest	Ctrl+Space	editor.action.triggerSuggest
Trigger Parameter Hints	Ctrl+Shift+Space	editor.action.triggerParameterHints
Format Document	Shift+Alt+F	editor.action.formatDocument
Format Selection	Ctrl+K Ctrl+F	editor.action.formatSelection
Go to Definition	F12	editor.action.revealDefinition
Show Hover	Ctrl+K Ctrl+I	editor.action.showHover
Peek Definition	Alt+F12	editor.action.peekDefinition
Open Definition to the Side	Ctrl+K F12	editor.action.revealDefinitionAside
Quick Fix	Ctrl+.	editor.action.quickFix
Go to References	Shift+F12	editor.action.goToReferences
Rename Symbol	F2	editor.action.rename
Replace with Next Value	Ctrl+Shift+.	editor.action.inPlaceReplace.down
Replace with Previous Value	Ctrl+Shift+,	editor.action.inPlaceReplace.up
Expand AST Selection	Shift+Alt+Right	editor.action.smartSelect.expand
Shrink AST Selection	Shift+Alt+Left	editor.action.smartSelect.shrink
Trim Trailing Whitespace	Ctrl+K Ctrl+X	editor.action.trimTrailingWhitespace
Change Language Mode	Ctrl+K M	workbench.action.editor.changeLanguageMode

Table 1-4. *Navigation*

Command	Key	Command id
Show All Symbols	Ctrl+T	workbench.action.showAllSymbols
Go to Line...	Ctrl+G	workbench.action.gotoLine
Go to File..., Quick Open	Ctrl+P	workbench.action.quickOpen
Go to Symbol...	Ctrl+Shift+O	workbench.action.gotoSymbol
Show Problems	Ctrl+Shift+M	workbench.actions.view.problems
Go to Next Error or Warning	F8	editor.action.marker.nextInFiles
Go to Previous Error or Warning	Shift+F8	editor.action.marker.prevInFiles
Show All Commands	Ctrl+Shift+P or F1	workbench.action.showCommands
Navigate Editor History	Ctrl+Tab	workbench.action.quickOpen PreviousRecentlyUsedEditorInGroup
Go Back	Alt+Left	workbench.action.navigateBack
Go back in Quick Input	Alt+Left	workbench.action.quickInputBack
Go Forward	Alt+Right	workbench.action.navigateForward

Table 1-5. *Editor/window management*

Command	Key	Command id
New Window	Ctrl+Shift+N	workbench.action.newWindow
Close Window	Ctrl+W	workbench.action.closeWindow
Close Editor	Ctrl+F4	workbench.action.closeActiveEditor
Close Folder	Ctrl+K F	workbench.action.closeFolder

(*continued*)

Table 1-5. (*continued*)

Command	Key	Command id
Cycle Between Editor Groups	unassigned	workbench.action .navigateEditorGroups
Split Editor	Ctrl+\	workbench.action.splitEditor
Focus into First Editor Group	Ctrl+1	workbench.action .focusFirstEditorGroup
Focus into Second Editor Group	Ctrl+2	workbench.action .focusSecondEditorGroup
Focus into Third Editor Group	Ctrl+3	workbench.action .focusThirdEditorGroup
Focus into Editor Group on the Left	unassigned	workbench.action .focusPreviousGroup
Focus into Editor Group on the Right	unassigned	workbench.action.focusNextGroup
Move Editor Left	Ctrl+Shift+PageUp	workbench.action .moveEditorLeftInGroup
Move Editor Right	Ctrl+Shift+PageDown	workbench.action .moveEditorRightInGroup
Move Active Editor Group Left	Ctrl+K Left	workbench.action .moveActiveEditorGroupLeft
Move Active Editor Group Right	Ctrl+K Right	workbench.action .moveActiveEditorGroupRight
Move Editor into Next Group	Ctrl+Alt+Right	workbench.action .moveEditorToNextGroup
Move Editor into Previous Group	Ctrl+Alt+Left	workbench.action .moveEditorToPreviousGroup

Table 1-6. *File management*

Command	Key	Command id
New File	Ctrl+N	workbench.action.files.newUntitledFile
Open File...	Ctrl+O	workbench.action.files.openFile
Save	Ctrl+S	workbench.action.files.save
Save All	Ctrl+K S	saveAll
Save As...	Ctrl+Shift+S	workbench.action.files.saveAs
Close	Ctrl+F4	workbench.action.closeActiveEditor
Close Others	unassigned	workbench.action.closeOtherEditors
Close Group	Ctrl+K W	workbench.action.closeEditorsInGroup
Close Other Groups	unassigned	workbench.action .closeEditorsInOtherGroups
Close Group to Left	unassigned	workbench.action.closeEditorsToTheLeft
Close Group to Right	unassigned	workbench.action.closeEditorsToTheRight
Close All	Ctrl+K Ctrl+W	workbench.action.closeAllEditors
Reopen Closed Editor	Ctrl+Shift+T	workbench.action.reopenClosedEditor
Keep Open	Ctrl+K Enter	workbench.action.keepEditor
Copy Path of Active File	Ctrl+K P	workbench.action.files.copyPathOfActiveFile
Reveal Active File in Window	Ctrl+K R	workbench.action.files. revealActiveFileInWindows
Show Opened File in New Window	Ctrl+K	workbench.action.files. showOpenedFileInNewWindow
Compare Opened File With	unassigned	workbench.files.action.compareFileWith

Table 1-7. Display

Command	Key	Command id
Toggle Full Screen	F11	workbench.action.toggleFullScreen
Toggle Zen Mode	Ctrl+K Z	workbench.action.toggleZenMode
Leave Zen Mode	Escape	workbench.action.exitZenMode
Zoom in	Ctrl+=	workbench.action.zoomIn
Zoom out	Ctrl+-	workbench.action.zoomOut
Reset Zoom	Ctrl+Numpad0	workbench.action.zoomReset
Toggle Sidebar Visibility	Ctrl+B	workbench.action.toggleSidebarVisibility
Show Explorer / Toggle Focus	Ctrl+Shift+E	workbench.view.explorer
Show Search	Ctrl+Shift+F	workbench.view.search
Show Source Control	Ctrl+Shift+G	workbench.view.scm
Show Run	Ctrl+Shift+D	workbench.view.debug
Show Extensions	Ctrl+Shift+X	workbench.view.extensions
Show Output	Ctrl+Shift+U	workbench.action.output.toggleOutput
Quick Open View	Ctrl+Q	workbench.action.quickOpenView
Open New Command Prompt	Ctrl+Shift+C	workbench.action.terminal.openNativeConsole
Toggle Markdown Preview	Ctrl+Shift+V	markdown.showPreview
Open Preview to the Side	Ctrl+K V	markdown.showPreviewToSide
Toggle Integrated Terminal	Ctrl+`	workbench.action.terminal.toggleTerminal

Table 1-8. *Search*

Command	Key	Command id
Show Search	Ctrl+Shift+F	workbench.view.search
Replace in Files	Ctrl+Shift+H	workbench.action.replaceInFiles
Toggle Match Case	Alt+C	toggleSearchCaseSensitive
Toggle Match Whole Word	Alt+W	toggleSearchWholeWord
Toggle Use Regular Expression	Alt+R	toggleSearchRegex
Toggle Search Details	Ctrl+Shift+J	workbench.action.search .toggleQueryDetails
Focus Next Search Result	F4	search.action.focusNextSearchResult
Focus Previous Search Result	Shift+F4	search.action.focusPreviousSearchResult
Show Next Search Term	Down	history.showNext
Show Previous Search Term	Up	history.showPrevious

Table 1-9. *Search editor*

Command	Key	Command id
Open Results In Editor	Alt+Enter	search.action.openInEditor
Focus Search Editor Input	Escape	search.action.focusQueryEditorWidget
Search Again	Ctrl+Shift+R	rerunSearchEditorSearch
Delete File Results	Ctrl+Shift+Backspace	search.searchEditor.action .deleteFileResults

Table 1-10. *Preferences*

Command	Key	Command id
Open Settings	Ctrl+,	workbench.action.openSettings
Open Workspace Settings	unassigned	workbench.action .openWorkspaceSettings
Open Keyboard Shortcuts	Ctrl+K Ctrl+S	workbench.action .openGlobalKeybindings
Open User Snippets	unassigned	workbench.action.openSnippets
Select Color Theme	Ctrl+K Ctrl+T	workbench.action.selectTheme
Configure Display Language	unassigned	workbench.action.configureLocale

Table 1-11. *Debug*

Command	Key	Command id
Toggle Breakpoint	F9	editor.debug.action.toggleBreakpoint
Start	F5	workbench.action.debug.start
Continue	F5	workbench.action.debug.continue
Start (without debugging)	Ctrl+F5	workbench.action.debug.run
Pause	F6	workbench.action.debug.pause
Step Into	F11	workbench.action.debug.stepInto

Table 1-12. *Tasks*

Command	Key	Command id
Run Build Task	Ctrl+Shift+B	workbench.action.tasks.build
Run Test Task	Unassigned	workbench.action.tasks.test

Table 1-13. *Extensions*

Command	Key	Command id
Install Extension	unassigned	workbench.extensions .action.installExtension
Show Installed Extensions	unassigned	workbench .extensions.action .showInstalledExtensions
Show Outdated Extensions	unassigned	workbench .extensions.action .listOutdatedExtensions
Show Recommended Extensions	unassigned	workbench.extensions .action.showRecommended Extensions
Show Popular Extensions	unassigned	workbench .extensions.action .showPopularExtensions
Update All Extensions	unassigned	workbench.extensions .action.updateAllExtensions

Programming Languages Supported

In VS Code, there is a support tool for almost every major programming language. Most of the default settings for JavaScript, TypeScript, CSS, and HTML with rich language extensions can be found in the VS Code Marketplace. These are eight of the most popular language extensions:

- Python

- C/C++

- C#

- Java Extension Pack

- Go

- Dart

- PHP Extension Pack

- Ruby

You can go to the Marketplace or check out the integrated Extensions view and search for your desired programming language to find snippets, code completion and IntelliSense providers, linters, debuggers, and more. If you want to change the display language of VS Code (for example, to some other available language), you can do that in the Display Language topic.

It is best to have some prior understanding of these programming languages and their language specific documentation supported by VS Code in advance.

Language Features in VS Code

The richness of support characteristics varies across the different languages and their extensions:

- Syntax highlighting and bracket matching

- Smart completions

- Linting and corrections

- Code navigation (Go to Definition, Find All References)

- Debugging

- Refactoring

Changing the Language for the Selected File

In VS Code, there is a default setting of the language support for a file based on its filename extension. Nevertheless, when you need to change a few language modes, you can do so by clicking on the language indicator, which is located on the right-hand side of the Status Bar. This will call up the Select Language Mode dropdown, where you can see and choose another language for the current file.

Additional Components and Tools

VS Code is quite minimal by design and only includes the limited number of components shared across most development platforms. Basic functionality such as the editor, file management, window management, and preference settings are included. A JavaScript and TypeScript language service and Node.js debugger are also part of the basic structure.

If you are used to working with bigger, more inclusive, and diverse development tools, you may be surprised that your scenarios are not always fully supported out of the box. For instance, there is not a File ➤ New Project dialog with preinstalled project templates. Most VS Code users will be required to look for and download additional components, depending on their specific projects.

Commonly Used Components

Here are a few commonly installed components:

- **Git:** VS Code has built-in support for source code control using Git, but needs Git to be installed on the side.

- **Node.js (includes npm):** A cross-platform mostly used for building and running JavaScript applications.

- **TypeScript:** The TypeScript compiler, tsc, for transcripting TypeScript to JavaScript.

VS Code Extensions

You can also expand the VS Code editor itself through extensions. The VS Code community has built the multiple varieties of useful extensions available on the VS Code Marketplace for the following programming languages:

- Python
- C/C++
- Jupyter
- ESLint
- Prettier: code formatter
- Live Server
- Visual Studio IntelliCode
- C#

Additional Tools

VS Code effectively integrates with some widely used toolchains. The following tools will assist in advancing your development experience:

- **Yeoman:** an application scaffolding tool, a command-line version of File ➤ New Project.

- **generator-aspnet:** a Yeoman generator for running ASP.NET Core applications.

- **generator-hot towel:** a Yeoman generator for easy creation of AngularJS applications.

- **Express:** an application framework for Node.js applications using the Pug template engine.

- **Gulp:** a streaming task runner system that could be incorporated with VS Code tasks.

- **Mocha:** a JavaScript test framework that runs on Node.js.

- **Yarn:** a dependency manager and a good alternative to npm.

Please note that most of these tools require Node.js and the npm package manager to download and apply.

Settings Precedence

Configurations can be overridden at multiple levels by the different setting scopes:

> **User settings:** applies globally to all VS Code instances.
>
> **Workspace setting:** goes to the open folder or workspace and normally overrides User settings.
>
> **Workspace Folder settings:** typically applies to a specific folder of a multiroot workspace; overrides both User and Workspace settings.

Setting values can be of various types:

- **String:** "files.autoSave": "afterDelay"

- **Boolean:** "editor.minimap.enabled": true

- **Number:** "files.autoSaveDelay": 1000

- **Array:** "editor.rulers": []

- **Object:** "search.exclude": { "**/node_modules": true, "**/bower_components": true }

Values with primitive types and Array type are overridden, but those with Object type are merged. For example, workbench. colorCustomizations takes an Object that specifies a group of User Interface items and their desired colors. If there are conflicting values, the usual reaction would be to override behavior with workspace values taking precedence over user values.

Settings and Security

Some settings let you specify an executable that VS Code will run to operate over certain operations. For example, you can select which shell the Integrated Terminal would be using. For more advanced security, such settings can only be determined in user settings and not at workspace scope. See the list of settings not supported in workspace settings:

- git.path

- terminal.external.windowsExec

- terminal.external.osxExec

- terminal.external.linuxExec

The first time you activate a workspace that determines any of these settings, VS Code is going to warn you once, and you may ignore the values after that.

Summary

In this chapter we have covered the basics related to VS Code, including its user interface and keyboard shortcuts.

In the next chapter we will look closer at the VS Code for Python Development, including the list of required extensions, linting, and debugging requirements.

CHAPTER 2

Getting Started with Python Programs in Visual Studio Code

In the previous chapter, we covered the basics of VS Code. In this chapter, we are going to explain how to set up your VS Code for Python development. It can be easily downloaded and installed for all the major operating systems such as Windows, Linux, and macOS.

Installation Basics

First, let's cover the installation basics.

For the sake of illustrating examples, we are going to show how to install most of the tools on Windows. Windows will be used as the development environment for setting up the Python environment. For Linux and macOS, the process will be almost the same; nevertheless, there are a few differences in the commands.

All you have to do to start is to navigate to `https://code.visualstudio.com/download` and choose the appropriate platform to install the software. Once the download is completed, proceed with the normal installation.

© Sufyan bin Uzayr 2021
S. bin Uzayr, *Optimizing Visual Studio Code for Python Development*,
https://doi.org/10.1007/978-1-4842-7344-9_2

Once VS Code is up and running, the next thing to do is to set up the Python runtime environment. Again, you can install Python on all three operating systems (Windows, Linux, and macOS). Once Python has been downloaded and installed, you can go to the command prompt and run the following commands to verify whether the installation has been successful or not. To verify that you have installed Python successfully on your machine, activate one of the following commands (depending on your operating system):

- **Linux and macOS:** open a Terminal Window and type the following command:

  ```
  python3 --version
  ```

- **Windows:** open a command prompt and run the following command:

  ```
  py -3 --version
  ```

If the installation was successful, the output window should be able to display the version of Python that you installed.

Next, we will learn to install extensions for VS Code.

Reviewing the Required Extensions

By default, VS Code operates just like an ordinary text editor and does not have any built-in support for Python. What this means is that even though you can easily write Python code in VS Code, you will not be able to upgrade and use some of the developer tools or techniques that make writing code a lot easier. VS Code supports development in multiple programming languages through a well-documented extension model. The Python extension enables Python development in VS Code, with the following features:

- Support for Python 3.4 and higher, as well as Python 2.7

- Code completion with IntelliSense

- Linting

- Debugging support

- Code snippets

- Unit testing support

- Automatic use of virtual environments

- Code editing in Jupyter environments and Jupyter Notebooks

- Installing the Python extension for VS Code

VS Code extensions also cover more than just programming language capabilities:

- Keymaps let users already familiar with Atom, Sublime Text, Emacs, Vim, PyCharm, or other environments advance your coding.

- Themes customize the User Interface, whether you like coding in the light, dark, or something more colorful.

- Language packs let you have a more localized experience.

- GitLens has tons of useful Git features directly in your editing platform, including blame annotations and repository exploration features.

- Autosave is easily turned on by selecting File, AutoSave from the menu. The default delay time is 1000 milliseconds, which is also adjustable.

- Settings Sync offers to synchronize your VS Code settings across different installations using GitHub. If you work on different machines, this is useful to keep your environment consistent across all of them.

- Docker lets you quickly and easily work with Docker, helping author Dockerfile and docker-compose. yml, setting and deploying your projects, and even producing the proper Docker files for your project.

Identifying and installing additional extensions and themes is possible by clicking on the Extensions icon on the Activity Bar. You can look for extensions using keywords, sort the results in the most preferred ways, and install extensions quickly and effortlessly.

The following sections take a look in brief at the top eight extensions for Python in VS Code, visible by typing Python in the Extensions item on the Activity Bar. There are more extensions that developers like to use, but here we want to focus on the extensions that are applicable for Python only.

Tabnine

Tabnine is an extension that offers code completion suggestions based on a model that has millions of open-source code lines stored, which are then offered to the code you are currently working on. Tabnine sends minimal contextual data pieces from your currently edited file that allows us to make predictions based on your current project objectives. This extension does not use your code to train the core model, and the information sent to the server is only used to compute your prediction and is not being saved for any further application.

In addition, Tabnine is viewed as a powerful artificial intelligence (AI) assistant designed to help you code faster, prevent any mistakes, and get accustomed to the best coding practices without ever having to leave the comfort of VS Code. Tabnine studies publicly shared code and uses AI based learning algorithms that provide it with the ability to see your next coding requests and suggest one-click code completion. Tabnine works with all major programming languages, including JavaScript, Python, TypeScript, PHP, C/C++, HTML/CSS, Go, Java, Ruby, C#, Rust, SQL, Bash, Kotlin, Julia, Lua, OCaml, Perl, Haskell, and React.

Bracket Pair Colorizer

This extension allows matching brackets to be spotted or classified with colors. This way the user can determine which characters to match, and which colors to use. Here are the few basic settings:[1]

- **"bracketPairColorizer.timeOut":** configures how long the editor should be idle for before updating the document; set to 0 to disable.

- **"bracketPairColorizer.forceUniqueOpeningColor":** disabled.

- **"bracketPairColorizer.forceIterationColorCycle":** enabled.

- **"bracketPairColorizer.colorMode":** consecutive brackets share a color pool for all bracket types.

    Independent brackets allow each bracket type to use its own color pool:

- **"bracketPairColorizer.highlightActiveScope":** highlights currently scoped brackets.

---

[1] Visual Studio Code, "Bracket Pair Colorizer," https://marketplace. visualstudio.com/items?itemName=CoenraadS.bracket-pair-colorizer, accessed July 29, 2021.

- **"bracketPairColorizer.activeScopeCSS":** chooses a border style to highlight the active scope; use {color} to match the existing bracket color. It is recommended to disable the inbuilt editor.matchBrackets setting if using this feature. Add the value "backgroundColor : {color}" to increase visibility.

- **"bracketPairColorizer.showBracketsInGutter":** shows active scope brackets in the gutter.

- **"bracketPairColorizer.showBracketsInRuler":** shows active scope brackets in the ruler.

- **"bracketPairColorizer.rulerPosition":** decoration position in the ruler.

- **"bracketPairColorizer.showVerticalScopeLine":** shows a vertical line between the brackets.

- **"bracketPairColorizer.showHorizontalScopeLine":** shows a horizontal line between the brackets; enabled by default

- **"bracketPairColorizer.scopeLineRelativePosition":** disable to show the vertical line in column 0.

- **"bracketPairColorizer.scopeLineCSS":** chooses a border style to highlight the active scope; use {color} to match the existing bracket color.

- **"bracketPairColorizer.consecutivePairColors":** a new bracket pair can be configured by adding it to the array. Note: Pair must be supported punctuation type by Prism.js.

- **"bracketPairColorizer.independentPairColors":** a new bracket pair can be configured by adding it to the array. Note: Pair must be supported punctuation type by Prism.js

- **"bracketPairColorizer.excludedLanguages":** excludes languages from being parsed by this extension.

Python Snippets

A snippet set is there in the Marketplace to make you more efficient working with Python. By default, the standard snippet pack contains all of the following Python methods:

- all Python built-in snippets and contains at least one example for each method

- all Python string snippets contain at least one example for each method

- all Python list snippets contain at least one example for each method

- all Python sets snippets contain at least one example for each method

- all Python tuple snippets contain at least one example for each method

- all Python dictionary snippets contain at least one example for each method

In addition, the set also contains a lot of other code snippets like if/else, for, while, while/else, try/catch, file process, class snippets, and others,[2] as shown in Table 2-1.

---

[2] Visual Studio Code, "Python Snippets," https://marketplace.visualstudio.com/items?itemName=cstrap.python-snippets, accessed July 29, 2021.

Table 2-1. *Additional code snippets*

Snippets	Descriptons
abs	Returns the absolute value of a number
all	Returns True if all items in an iterable object are true
any	Returns True if any item in an iterable object is true
ASCII	Returns a readable version of an object. Replaces none-ASCII characters with escape character
bin	Returns the binary version of a number
bool	Returns the Boolean value of the specified object
bytearray	Returns an array of bytes
bytes	Returns a bytes object
callable	Returns True if the specified object is callable, otherwise False
chr	Returns a character from the specified Unicode code.
delattr	Deletes the specified attribute (property or method) from the specified object
dict	Returns a dictionary (Array)
dir	Returns a list of the specified object's properties and methods
divmod	Returns the quotient and the remainder when argument1 is divided by argument2
enumerate	Takes a collection (e.g., a tuple) and returns it as an enumerate object
eval	Evaluates and executes an expression
exec	Executes the specified code (or object)
filter	Use a filter function to exclude items in an iterable object
float	Returns a floating-point number
frozenset	Returns a frozenset object

(continued)

Table 2-1. (*continued*)

Snippets	Descriptons
getattr	Returns the value of the specified attribute (property or method)
globals	Returns the current global symbol table as a dictionary
hasattr	Returns True if the specified object has the specified attribute (property/method)
hash	Returns the hash value of a specified object
help	Executes the built-in help system
hex	Converts a number into a hexadecimal value
int	Returns an integer number
id	Returns the id of an object
input	Allowing user input
isinstance	Returns True if a specified object is an instance of a specified object
issubclass	Returns True if a specified class is a subclass of a specified object
iter	Returns an iterator object
len	Returns the length of an object
locals	Returns an updated dictionary of the current local symbol table
map	Returns the specified iterator with the specified function applied to each item
max	Returns the largest item in an iterable
memoryview	Returns a memory view object
min	Returns the smallest item in an iterable
next	Returns the next item in an iterable
object	Returns a new object
oct	Converts a number into an octal

(*continued*)

Table 2-1. (*continued*)

Snippets	Descriptons
open	Opens a file and returns a file object
ord	Given a string of length one, return an integer representing the Unicode code point of the character when the argument is a Unicode object, or the value of the byte when the argument is an 8-bit string.
pow	Return x to the power y
print	Prints to the standard output device
property	Gets, sets, deletes a property
range	returns a sequence of numbers, starting from 0 and increments by 1 (by default)
repr	Returns a readable version of an object
reversed	Returns a reversed iterator
round	Rounds a numbers
slice	Returns a slice object
sorted	Returns a sorted list
staticmethod	Converts a method into a static method
str	Returns a string object
sum	Sums the items of an iterator
super	Return a proxy object that delegates method calls to a parent or sibling class of type.
type	Returns the type of an object
unichr	Return the Unicode string of one character whose Unicode code is the integer i.
vars	Returns the dict property of an object
zip	Returns an iterator, from two or more iterators

Python Test Explorer for Visual Studio Code

This extension offers you an option to run your Python Unittest or Pytest tests with the Test Explorer UI. Moreover, the extension lets you operate your Python tests in the sidebar of VS Code. There are some key features that make it highly popular among developers:

- Displays a Test Explorer in the Test view in VS Code's sidebar with all noticed tests and suites and their condition.

- Convenient error reporting function during the testing.

- Unittest and Pytest debugging.

- Notifies about the failed test's log when the test is selected in the explorer.

- Supports multiroot workspaces.

- Supports Unittest and Pytest test frameworks and their plugins.

- Comparison to Python extension's Test View.

- Better error reporting during the discovery stage. If there are errors, you will see such tests in an errored state, and by clicking on them, a complete error message would be displayed in the Output panel. Python Extension, at best, will not show your tests that contain errors such as syntax errors or invalid data.

- Tends to work better with pytest plugins such as Tavern. Python Extension will not recognize these tests.

- Based on Test Explorer User Interface. This fact may be particularly handy when you have a workspace with projects in different languages or frameworks. Test Explorer User Interface has a lot of plugins, and you can conveniently discover and run tests at the same View.

- Shows your errors and a complete report of your tests by clicking on a failed test.

- Has only relevant folders from your workspace on the platform display. Showing all workspace folders, as the Python Extension is doing, can be slightly problematic when you have multiple workspace folders, but only a couple of them have any tests.

User experience with both extensions is highly subjective. However, you might prefer the user interface of this extension better. Also, each discovery, test execution, and test cancellation won't require you to select a folder when you have multiple in your workspace.

By default, the extension configuration uses the configuration from Python extension for VS Code. To modify Python for your project, see Getting Started with Python in VS Code. Nevertheless, test framework applied by this extension can be overridden by the pythonTestExplorer. testFramework configuration property. The two available options are unittest and pytest. When property is set to null, the configuration from Python extension is used.

When configuring Python test discovery and execution, make sure you are familiar with the list of currently used properties shown in Table 2-2.[3]

---

[3] Visual Studio Code, "Python Test Explorer for Visual Studio Code," https://marketplace.visualstudio.com/items?itemName=LittleFoxTeam. vscode-python-test-adapter, accessed July 29, 2021.

Table 2-2. *Properties used in VS Code for Python development*

Property	Description
python.pythonPath	Path to Python.
python.envFile	Path to environment variable definitions file.
python.testing.cwd	Optional working directory for unit tests.
python.testing.unittestEnabled	Whether to enable or disable unit testing using unittest (enables or disables test discovery for Test Explorer).
python.testing.unittestArgs	Arguments used for test discovery (currently only -s and -p arguments are considered).
python.testing.pyTestEnabled	Whether to enable or disable unit testing using pytest (enables or disables test discovery for Test Explorer).
python.testing.pytestPath	Path to pytest executable or a pytest compatible module.
python.testing.pyTestArgs	Arguments passed to the pytest. Each argument is a separate item in the array.
python.testing .autoTestDiscoverOnSaveEnabled	When true tests will be automatically rediscovered when saving a text file.
pythonTestExplorer.testFramework	Test framework to use (overrides Python extension properties python.testing .unittestEnabled and python.testing .pyTestEnabled).

The configurations in Table 2-2 support placeholders for workspace folder as ${workspaceFolder} and environment variables in a form of ${env:YOUR_ENVIRONMENT_VARIABLE}.

If you are configuring Test Explorer User Interface, use the g configuration properties listed in Table 2-3.[4]

Table 2-3. *Configuration properties*

Property	Description
testExplorer.onStart	Retire or reset all test states whenever a test run is started
testExplorer.onReload	Retire or reset all test states whenever the test tree is reloaded
testExplorer.codeLens	Show a CodeLens above each test or suite for running or debugging the tests
testExplorer .gutterDecoration	Show the state of each test in the editor using Gutter Decorations
testExplorer .errorDecoration	Show error messages from test failures as decorations in the editor
testExplorer .errorDecorationHover	Provide hover messages for the error decorations in the editor
testExplorer.sort	Sort the tests and suites by label or location. If this is not set (or set to null), they will be shown in the order that they were received from the adapter
testExplorer .showCollapseButton	Show a button for collapsing the nodes of the test tree
testExplorer .showExpandButton	Show a button for expanding the top nodes of the test tree, recursively for the given number of levels

(*continued*)

---

[4]Visual Studio Code, "Python Test Explorer for Visual Studio Code."

Table 2-3. (*continued*)

Property	Description
testExplorer.showOnRun	Switch to the Test Explorer view whenever a test run is started
testExplorer .addToEditorContextMenu	Add menu items for running and debugging the tests in the current file to the editor context menu
testExplorer.mergeSuites	Merge suites with the same label and parent
testExplorer.hideEmptyLog	Hide the output channel used to show a test's log when the user clicks on a test whose log is empty
testExplorer.hideWhen	Hide the Test Explorer when no test adapters have been registered or when no tests have been found by the registered adapters. The default is to never hide the Test Explorer and there are some test adapters only work with this default setting.

Configuring Debug

This extension typically searches for a configuration in launch.json with "type": "python" and "request": "test" to load any of the following items during debugging:

- name
- console
- env
- componentry
- showReturnValue
- redirectOutput
- debugStdLib

- justMyCode

- subProcess

- envFile

Better Comments

The Better Comments extension is there to help you create more user-friendly, informative comments in your code. Extension can also assist you to able to categorise your annotations into Alerts, Queries, TODOs, and Project Highlights. Commented out code can also be styled in any way you like to make it clear what the code's objective is, and any other comment styles you would like can be tuned in the settings. This extension can also be configured in the following manner in User Settings or Workspace settings:[5]

- **"better-comments.multilineComments"**: true

   This setting will control whether multiline comments are styled using the annotation tags. When false, multiline comments will be presented without decoration.

- **"better-comments.highlightPlainText"**: false

   This setting will control whether comments in a plain text file are styled using the annotation tags. When true, the tags (defaults: ! * ? //) will be detected if they're the first character on a line.

- **better-comments.tags:**

   The tags are the characters or sequences used to mark a comment for decoration. The default 5 can be modified to change the colors, and more can be added.

---

[5] Visual Studio Code, "Better Comments," `https://marketplace.visualstudio.com/items?itemName=aaron-bond.better-comments`, accessed July 29, 2021.

The list of the extension supported Languages is quite impressive and includes the following: Ada, AL, Apex, AsciiDoc, BrightScript, C, C#, C++, ColdFusion, Clojure, COBOL, CoffeeScript, CSS, Dart, Dockerfile, Elixir, Elm, Erlang, F#, Fortran, gdscript, GenStat, Go, GraphQL, Groovy, Haskell, Haxe, HiveQL, HTML, Java, JavaScript, JavaScript React, JSON with comments, Julia, Kotlin, LaTex (inlc. Bibtex/Biblatex), Less, Lisp, Lua, Makefile, Markdown, Nim, MATLAB, Objective-C, Objective-C++, Pascal, Perl, Perl 6, PHP, Pig, PlantUML, PL/SQL, PowerShell, Puppet, Python, R, Racket, Ruby, Rust, SAS, Sass, Scala, SCSS, ShaderLab, ShellScript, SQL, STATA, Stylus, Swift, Tcl, Terraform, Twig, TypeScript, TypeScript React, Verilog, Visual Basic, Vue.js, XML, and YAML.

AutoDocstring

This VS Code extension enables users to quickly generate docstrings for Python functions. It has some very useful features that include:

- Generation of docstring snippet that can be tabbed through.

- Developers can choose between several different types of docstring formats.

- Infers parameter types through pep484 type hints, default values, and var names.

- The extension supports args, kwargs, decorators, errors, and parameter types.

By default, autoDocstring supports the following docstring formats:

- Google

- docBlockr

- Numpy

- Sphinx

- PEP0257

When using the extension, it is recommended that some of the standard application rules be followed:

- Place the cursor on the line directly below the definition to generate full auto-populated docstring

- Make sure you press enter after opening docstring with triple quotes (" or ")

- Keyboard shortcut: ctrl+shift+2 or cmd+shift+2 for mac

- Can be changed in Preferences ➤ Keyboard Shortcuts ➤ extension.generateDocstring

- Command: Generate Docstring

- Right-click menu: Generate Docstring

This extension contributes the following settings:[6]

- **autoDocstring.docstringFormat:** Switch between different docstring formats

- **autoDocstring.customTemplatePath:** Path to a custom docstring template (absolute or relative to the project root)

- **autoDocstring.generateDocstringOnEnter:** Generate the docstring on pressing enter after opening docstring

- **autoDocstring.includeExtendedSummary:** Include extended summary section in docstring

- **autoDocstring.includeName:** Include function name at the start of docstring

---

[6]Visual Studio Code, "VSCode Python Docstring Generator," `https://marketplace.visualstudio.com/items?itemName=njpwerner.autodocstring`, accessed July 29, 2021.

- **autoDocstring.startOnNewLine:** Newline before summary placeholder

- **autoDocstring.guessTypes:** Infer types from type hints, default values and variable names

- **autoDocstring.quoteStyle:** The style of quotes for docstrings

This extension also supports custom templates with the help of the mustache.js templating engine. In order to use a custom template, you need to create a .mustache file and specify its path using the customTemplatePath configuration. You can take a look at the following tags that are available for use in custom templates:[7]

```
{{name}} - name of the function
{{summaryPlaceholder}} - [summary] placeholder
{{extendedSummaryPlaceholder}} - [extended_summary] placeholder

Sections
{{#args}} - iterate over function arguments
    {{var}} - variable name
    {{typePlaceholder}} - [type] or guessed type placeholder
    {{descriptionPlaceholder}} - [description] placeholder
{{/args}}

{{#kwargs}} - iterate over function kwargs
    {{var}} - variable name
    {{typePlaceholder}} - [type] or guessed type placeholder
    {{&default}} - default value (& unescapes the variable)
    {{descriptionPlaceholder}} - [description] placeholder
{{/kwargs}}
```

---

[7] Visual Studio Code, "VSCode Python Docstring Generator."

```
{{#exceptions}} - iterate over exceptions
    {{type}} - exception type
    {{descriptionPlaceholder}} - [description] placeholder
{{/exceptions}}

{{#yields}} - iterate over yields
    {{typePlaceholder}} - [type] placeholder
    {{descriptionPlaceholder}} - [description] placeholder
{{/yields}}

{{#returns}} - iterate over returns
    {{typePlaceholder}} - [type] placeholder
    {{descriptionPlaceholder}} - [description] placeholder
{{/returns}}

Additional Sections
{{#argsExist}} - display contents if args exist
{{/argsExist}}

{{#kwargsExist}} - display contents if kwargs exist
{{/kwargsExist}}

{{#parametersExist}} - display contents if args or kwargs exist
{{/parametersExist}}

{{#exceptionsExist}} - display contents if exceptions exist
{{/exceptionsExist}}

{{#yieldsExist}} - display contents if returns exist
{{/yieldsExist}}

{{#returnsExist}} - display contents if returns exist
{{/returnsExist}}
{{#placeholder}} - makes contents a placeholder
```

Python Indent

This Extension helps quickly generate docstrings for Python functions. Any time you press the Enter key in a Python context, this extension will parse your Python file up to the place of your cursor, and define exactly how much the next line (or two in the case of hanging indents) should be indented and how much close bylines should be un-indented.

In the next section, we will now start off with code editing in VS Code.

Getting Started with Code Editing

VS Code editing should start by an explanation of what IntelliSense is. It is a general term for various code editing features including code completion, parameter info, quick info, and member lists. IntelliSense features are also referred to by other names such as code completion, content assist, and code hinting.

VS Code IntelliSense is provided for JavaScript, TypeScript, JSON, HTML, CSS, and SCSS. VS Code supports word-based completions for any programming language but can as well be configured to have more extensive IntelliSense by installing a language extension.

Autocomplete and IntelliSense

Autocomplete together with IntelliSense is provided for all files within the currently activated folder and for Python packages that are installed in standard locations. During editing, you can right-click different identifiers to take advantage of several convenient commands:[8]

---

[8] Visual Studio Code, "Editing Python in Visual Studio Code," `https://code.visualstudio.com/docs/python/editing`, accessed July 29, 2021.

- Go to Definition (F12) transfers from your code into the code that defines an object. This command is useful when you are operating with libraries.

- Peek Definition (Alt+F12), is almost the same as the previous one but displays the definition directly in the editor (making space in the editor window to avoid messing any code). Press Escape to close the Peek window or use the x in the upper right corner.

- Go to Declaration jumps to the point at which the variable or other item is declared in your code.

- Peek Declaration is similar but displays the declaration directly in the editor. Again, you can use Escape or the x in the upper right corner to close the Peek window.

Customizing IntelliSense Behavior

To customize the behavior of the engine, you should check the code analysis settings and autocomplete settings. You can also customize the general behavior of autocomplete and IntelliSense, even to disable these tune-ins completely. IntelliCode provides a set of AI-assisted capabilities for IntelliSense in Python, such as inferring the most relevant auto-completions based on the current code context.

To enable IntelliSense for packages that are installed in other, nonstandard locations, add those locations to the python.autoComplete. extraPaths collection in the settings file (the default collection is empty). For example, you might already have installed Google App Engine in custom locations, specified in-app.yaml if you use Flask. In this case you would have to specify those locations in the following way:

Windows:

```
"python.autoComplete.extraPaths": [
    "C:/Program Files (x86)/Google/google_appengine",
    "C:/Program Files (x86)/Google/google_appengine/lib/
    flask-0.12"]
```

macOS/Linux:

```
"python.autoComplete.extraPaths": [
    "~/.local/lib/Google/google_appengine",
    "~/.local/lib/Google/google_appengine/lib/flask-0.12" ]
```

The python.autoComplete.addBrackets setting (default false) also defines whether VS Code automatically adds parentheses (()) when autocompleting a function name. For instance, when you set addBrackets to true:

```
"python.autoComplete.addBrackets": true,
```

and then write import os followed by os.getc, you will get autocomplete for os.getcwd. Selecting that auto-complete adds os.getcwd() to your source code and locates the cursor inside the parentheses. When the setting is false, only os.getcwd is added to the file.

Troubleshooting

If autocomplete and IntelliSense are not functioning for a custom module, it is advised to check the following causes:

- If the path to the Python interpreter is incorrect, check the pythonPath setting or restart VS Code if you make a correction.

- If the custom module is located in a nonstandard location or not installed using pip, be sure to add the location to the python.autoComplete.extraPaths setting and restart VS Code.

Running Selection/Line in Terminal (REPL)

The Python: Run Selection/Line in Python Terminal command (Shift+Enter) is the fastest way to take whatever code is selected, or the code on the current line if there is no selection, and run it in the Python Terminal. An identical Run Selection/Line in Python Terminal command can also be accessed on the context menu for a selection in the editor.

VS Code automatically deletes indents based on the first nonempty line of the selection, moving all other lines left accordingly. Source code that runs in the terminal/REPL is cumulative until the current instance of the terminal is finished. The command opens the Python Terminal only if needed; you can also start the interactive REPL environment directly using the Python via Start REPL command. If you are just starting to use Python: Run Selection/Line in Python Terminal command, VS Code will send the text to the REPL before that environment is ready, in which case the selection or line is not run. If you encounter this behavior, try the command again when the REPL has finished loading.

Formatting

Formatting makes code more user-friendly when applying specific rules and conventions for line spacing, indents, spacing around operators, and so on. At the same time, it does not really affect the functionality of the code itself. Linting, on the contrary, analyzes code for common syntactical, stylistic, and functional mistakes as well as unconventional programming practices that can result in errors. Even though there is a little overlap between formatting and linting, the two capabilities are operating complementarily.

The Python extension supports source code formatting using either autopep8 (the default), black, or yapf.

General Formatting Settings

Table 2-4 shows the general formatting setings for Python code in VS Code:

Table 2-4. *General formatting settings*

Setting (python.formatting.)	Default value	Description
Provider	"autopep8"	Specifies the formatter to use, either "autopep8", "yapf", or "black".

The settings in Table 2-5 apply mostly to the individual formatters. The Python extension looks in the current pythonPath for the formatter. In order to use a formatter in another location, be sure to specify that location in the designated custom path setting.

Table 2-5. *Formatter-specific settings*

Formatter	Install steps	Arguments setting (python.formatting.)	Custom path setting (python.formatting.)
autopep8	pip install pep8	autopep8Args	autopep8Path
	pip install -- upgrade autopep8		
black (see note)	pip install black	blackArgs	blackPath
Yapf	pip install yapf	yapfArgs	yapfPath

By default, you cannot install the Black formatter if a Python 2 environment is active. Trying to do so may display the message "Formatter black is not installed. Install?". If you try to install Black in response, another message appears stating, "Could not find a version that satisfies the requirement black. No matching distribution found for black."

To solve this issue and use the Black formatter with Python 2, first install Black in a Python 3 framework. Then set the python.formatting. blackPath setting to that install location. When using custom arguments, each top-level element of an argument string that is separated by space on the command line must be a separate item in the args list. To illustrate:

```
"python.formatting.autopep8Args": ["--max-line-length", "120",
"--experimental"],
"python.formatting.yapfArgs": ["--style",
"{based_on_style: chromium, indent_width: 20}"],
"python.formatting.blackArgs": ["--line-length", "100"]
```

Troubleshooting Your Formatting

If formatting attempts fails, check the potential causes listed in Table 2-6.[9]

Table 2-6. Troubleshooting formatting in VS Code

Cause	Solution
The path to the python interpreter is incorrect.	Check the pythonPath setting.

(continued)

---

[9]Visual Studio Code, "Editing Python in Visual Studio Code."

Table 2-6. (*continued*)

Cause	Solution
The formatter is not installed in the current environment.	Open a command prompt, navigate to the location specified in the pythonPath setting, and run pip install for the formatter.
The path to the formatter is incorrect.	Check the value of the appropriate python. formatting.<formatter>Path setting.
Custom arguments for the formatter are incorrect.	Check that the appropriate python.formatting.<formatter>Path setting does not contain arguments, and that python. formatting.<formatter>Args contains a list of individual top-level argument elements such as "python.formatting .yapfArgs": ["--style", "{based_on_style: chromium, indent_width: 20}"].

In cases when a warning message "Black does not support the Format Select" comes out, possible solution could be preventing it with the following settings "[python]": {"editor.formatOnPaste": false, "editor. formatOnSaveMode": "file"}.

Refactoring

The Python extension includes three refactoring commands: Extract Variable, Extract Method, and Sort Imports.

Extract Variable

Extracts all similar items of the selected text within the particular scope, and replaces it with a variable. The new method is given the name newvariableNNN where NNN stands for a random number. It is typically invoked by:

- Context Menu: right-click a selection and select Extract Variable.

- Command Palette (Ctrl+Shift+P), then Python Refactor: Extract Variable.

- Assign a keyboard shortcut to the python. refactorExtractVariable command.

Extract Method

Extracts all similar items of the particular expression or block within the current scope, and replaces it with a method call. The new method is given the name newmethodNNN where NNN stands for a random number. It is normally invoked by:

- Context Menu: right-click a selection and select Extract Method.

- Command Palette (Ctrl+Shift+P), then Python Refactor: Extract Method.

- Assign a keyboard shortcut to the python. refactorExtractMethod command.

- Refactoring code into a method.

Sort Imports

Sort Imports applies the sort package to set all specific imports from the same module into a single import statement and organize import statements in alphabetical order. It is typically invoked by:

- Right-click in the editor and select Sort Imports (no selection is required).

- Command Palette (Ctrl+Shift+P), then Python Refactor: Sort Imports.

- Assign a keyboard shortcut to the python.sortImports command.

- Sorting import statements.

Custom applications to sort are specified in the python.sortImports. args setting, where each top-level item, as divided by spaces on the command line, is a single item in the array:

"python.sortImports.args": ["-rc", "--atomic"]. In order to use a custom isort script, it is better to use the python.sortImports.path setting to set a specific path.

Linting

Linting is different from the previously mentioned Formatting method due to the fact that it analyzes how the code runs and traces errors while Formatting can only restructure how code is framed. Linting points out any syntactical and stylistic issues in your Python source code, which at most times helps you see and correct subtle programming mistakes or outdated coding practices that can result in errors. For instance, linting traces the use of an uninitialized or undetermined variable, requests to undefined functions, missing parentheses, and even more underlining issues, such as trying to redefine built-in types or functions.

By default, stylistic and syntactical code detection is completed by the Language Server. If you require third-party linters for additional problem detection, you can easily enable them by using the Python: Select Linter command and the appropriate linter. You can certainly enable and disable all linting by using the Python: Enable Linting function.

Enabling Linters

To turn on linters other than the default PyLint, you should open the Command Palette (Ctrl+Shift+P) and select the Python: Select Linter command. This command adds "python.linting.<linter>Enabled": true to your settings, where <linter> is the name of the selected linter. You can also See Specific linters for details and enable a linter prompts to install the required packages in your programming environment.

If you are using a global environment and VS Code is not running efficiently, linter installation may fail. In that case, either run VS Code elevated, or manually run the Python package manager to install the linter at an elevated command prompt for the same environment: for example, *sudo pip3 install pylint* (for macOS and Linux) or *pip install pylint* (for Windows).

Disabling Linting

You can disable all Python linting with the Python: Enable Linting command, which shows a dropdown with the current linting state and see the options to turn Python linting on or off.

Running Linting

To efficiently run linting you need to:

- Linting runs by default any time you save a file.

- Open the Command Palette (Ctrl+Shift+P), then enter and click on Python: Run Linting.

Should you face any issues, they all will be shown in the Problems panel and as underlines in the code editor.

Linting Settings

This section lists general and specific settings for linting. You are free to add any of the settings to your user settings.json file (go through the File ➤ Preferences ➤ Settings command Ctrl+,). You can also refer to User and Workspace settings to find out how to change the linting behavior across all enabled linters. You can modify the following settings in the Table 2-7:[10]

Table 2-7. Linting settings

Feature	Setting (python. linting.)	Default value
Linting in general	Enabled	True
Linting on file save	lintOnSave	True
Maximum number of linting messages	maxNumberOfProblems	100
Exclude file and folder patterns	ignorePatterns	[".vscode/*.py", "**/site-packages/**/*.py"]

You can easily change python.linting.enabled via Python as well by clicking on Enable Linting command. However, when enabling lintOnSave, you might also want to enable the generic files.autoSave option (Save / AutoSave). This function provides regular linting feedback in your code as you script it.

---

[10]Visual Studio Code, "Linting Python in Visual Studio Code," https://code. visualstudio.com/docs/python/linting, accessed July 29, 2021.

Specific Linters

Table 2-8 lists the available Python linters and their basic settings. Be sure to note that only Pylint is enabled by default.[11]

Table 2-8. *Available Python linters*

Linter	Package name	Default state	True/false enable setting (python. linting.)	Arguments setting (python. linting.)	Custom path setting (python. linting.)
Pylint (default)	pylint	Enabled	pylint Enabled	pylintArgs	pylintPath
Flake8	flake8	Disabled	flake8 Enabled	flake8Args	flake8Path
mypy	mypy	Disabled	mypy Enabled	mypyArgs	mypyPath
pydocstyle	pydocstyle	Disabled	pydocstyle Enabled	pydocstyle Args	pydocstyle Path
pycodestyle (pep8)	pycodestyle	Disabled	pycodestyle Enabled	pycodestyle Args	pycodestyle Path
prospector	prospector	Disabled	prospector Enabled	prospector Args	prospector Path
pylama	pylama	Disabled	pylama Enabled	pylama Args	pylamaPath
bandit	bandit	Disabled	bandit Enabled	bandit Args	banditPath

[11] Visual Studio Code, "Linting Python in Visual Studio Code."

To choose a different linter, it is useful to do it through the Python: Select Linter command. You can also edit your settings manually to enable multiple linters. At the same time, keep in mind that applying the Select Linter command will overwrite those edits. Custom arguments are predetermined in the appropriate arguments setting for each linter. Each top-level element of an argument string that is separated by a space on the command line should be a separate item in the arguments (args) list. However, if a top-level element is a single value, as delineated by quotation marks or braces, it still comes out as a single item in the list even if the value itself has spaces.

A custom path is not usually needed, as the Python extension has the path to the linter based on the applied Python interpreter. To use a different version of a linter, write down its path in the specified custom path setting. For instance, if your selected interpreter is a virtual environment but you want to use a linter that is installed in a global environment, you will have to set the appropriate path setting to point to the global environment's linter.

Pylint

Pylint messages fall into the types listed in Table 2-9, with the indicated mapping to VS Code categories. You can modify the setting if you want to change the mapping.[12]

---

[12] Visual Studio Code, "Linting Python in Visual Studio Code."

Table 2-9. *Pylint categories with VS Code category mapping*

Pylint category	Description	VS Code category mapping	Applicable setting (python.linting.)
Convention (C)	Programming standard violation	Information (green underline)	pylintCategorySeverity. convention
Refactor (R)	Bad code smell	Hint (light bulbs)	pylintCategorySeverity. refactor
Warning (W)	Python-specific problems	Warning	pylintCategorySeverity. warning
Error (E)	Likely code bugs	Error (red underline)	pylintCategorySeverity. error
Fatal (F)	An error prevented further Pylint processing	Error	pylintCategorySeverity.fatal

Default Pylint Rules

Python in VS Code is customized by default to apply a set of three main linting rules that are relevant to the largest number of Python developers:[13]

- Enable all Error (E) and Fatal (F) messages.

- Disable all Convention (C) and Refactor (R) messages

- Disable all Warning (W) messages, except the following:

  - unreachable (W0101): Unreachable code

  - duplicate-key (W0109): Duplicate key %r in the dictionary

---

[13] Visual Studio Code, "Linting Python in Visual Studio Code."

- unnecessary-semicolon (W0301): Unnecessary semicolon

- global-variable-not-assigned (W0602): Using global for %r but no assignment is completed

- unused-variable (W0612): Unused variable %r

- binary-op-exception (W0711): Exception to catch is the result of a binary "%s" operation

- bad-format-string (W1302): Invalid format string

- anomalous-backslash-in-string (W1401): Anomalous backslash in string

- bad-open-mode (W1501): "%s" is not a valid model for open

These rules are activated through the following default arguments passed to Pylint:

```
--disable=all, --enable=F, E, unreachable,duplicate-key,
unnecessary-semicolon,global-variable-not-assigned,
unused-variable,binary-op-exception,bad-format-string,
anomalous-backslash-in-string,bad-open-mode
```

These items are passed every time the python.linting .pylintUseMinimalCheckers is set to true. But if you specify a value in pylintArgs or use a Pylint configuration file, then pylintUseMinimalCheckers is going to always be set to false.

In addition, command-line arguments can be used to load Pylint plugins, such as the plugin for Django:

```
"python.linting.pylintArgs": ["--load-plugins",
"pylint_django"]
```

Other options can also be specified in a pylintrc or .pylintrc options file in the workspace folder, as described on Pylint command line arguments.

Troubleshooting Linting

In Table 2-10, some of the basic error messages and their probable solutions are listed.[14]

Table 2-10. *Troubleshooting linting problems*

Error message	Cause	Solution
... unable to import <module_ name>	The Python extension is using the wrong version of Pylint.	Make sure that the `pythonPath` setting points to a valid Python installation where Pylint is installed. Also try setting the `python.linting.pylintPath` to an appropriate version of Pylint for the Python interpreter being used.
Linting with <linter> failed ...	The path to the Python interpreter is incorrect.	Check the `pythonPath` setting.
	The linter has not been installed in the current Python environment.	Open a command window, navigate to the location of the Python interpreter in the `pythonPath` setting, and run `pip install` for the linter.
	The path to the linter is incorrect.	Ensure that the appropriate `python.linting .<linter>Path` setting for the linter is correct.

(*continued*)

---

[14] Visual Studio Code, "Linting Python in Visual Studio Code."

Table 2-10. (*continued*)

Error message	Cause	Solution
	Custom arguments are defined incorrectly.	Check the appropriate `python.linting` `.<linter>Args` settings, and that the value of the setting is a list of the argument elements that are separated by spaces. For example, `"python.linting.pylintPath"`: `"pylint --load-plugins pylint_ django"` is incorrect. The correct syntax is `"python.linting.pylintArgs"`: `["--load-plugins", "pylint_django"]`

Debugging

Debugging refers to fixing your code and removing potential errors. Python is a syntactically typed language, which means that the role of your code editor becomes paramount in debugging, as a good editor can help you locate issues with your code in no time.

VS Code handles debugging on two fronts. On one hand, there are VS Code general debugging features such as inspecting variables, setting breakpoints, and others that are typically language-dependent; on the other hand, there are debugging considerations that are Python-specific debugging configurations, including specific app types and remote debugging.

Initializing Configurations

In order to initialize debug configurations, you have to first select the Run view in the sidebar and then press the Run icon. Configuration drives VS Code's behavior during a debugging session and is defined in a launch. json file that is stored in a .vscode folder in your workspace. To change debugging configuration, you need to make sure your code is stored in a folder.

If you do not yet have any configurations defined, you can see a button to Run and Debug and a link to create a configuration (launch. json) file: Debug toolbar settings command. To generate a launch.json file with Python configurations, complete the following steps: first, click the create a launch.json file link or use the Run ➤ Open configurations menu command. A configuration menu will be displayed from the Command Palette, offering you to choose the type of debug configuration you want for the opened file. Next, in the Select a debug configuration menu that appears, select Python File.Debug configurations menu.

Keep in mind that starting a debugging session through the Debug Panel, F5, or Run ➤ Start Debugging when no configuration exists will also bring up the debug configuration menu, but will not create a launch.json file.

The Python extension then generates and opens a launch.json file that has a predefined configuration based on what you previously selected—in this case, Python File. You can customize those configurations (by adding arguments, for instance), and also add custom configurations.

Additional Configurations

By default, VS Code displays only the most applied configurations provided by the Python extension. You can select other configurations to include in launch.json by activating the Add Configuration command shown in the list and in the launch.json editor. When you use the command, VS Code prompts you with a list of all available configurations (scroll down to see all the Python options):

- Adding a new Python debugging configuration

- Selecting the Node.js: Gulp task yields the following result:Added a configuration

- See Debugging specific app types for details on all of these configurations

During debugging, the Status Bar will present the current configuration and the current debugging interpreter. Selecting the configuration calls up a list from which you can select a different configuration. Normally, the debugger uses the same python.pythonPath workspace setting as for other features of VS Code. To apply a different interpreter for debugging specifically, you need to set the value for python in launch.json for the applicable debugger configuration. As an alternative, you can select the named interpreter on the Status Bar to opt for a different one.

Basic Debugging

The easiest way to start debugging a Python file is to use the Run view and click the Run and Debug icon. If no configuration has been previously done, you will be presented with a list of debugging options. You simply need to select the appropriate option to quickly begin debugging your code.

The two most used options are Python File configuration to operate the currently open Python file, and the Attach to use with Process ID to add the debugger to a process that is already running. Once a configuration is added, it can be selected from the dropdown list and started using the Start Debugging button. Additionally, you can also add other settings such as args that are not included in the standard configurations:[15]

---

[15] Visual Studio Code, "Python Debugging in VS Code," https://code.
visualstudio.com/docs/python/debugging, accessed July 29, 2021.

- **name:** Provides the name for the debug configuration that appears in the VS Code dropdown list.

- **type:** Identifies the type of debugger to use; leave this set to Python for Python code.

- **request:** Specifies the mode in which to start debugging:

  - **launch:** start the debugger on the file specified in program

  - **attach:** attach the debugger to an already running process. See Remote debugging for an example.

  - **program:** Provides the fully qualified path to the Python program's entry module. The value ${file}, often used in default configurations, uses the currently active file in the editor. By specifying a specific startup file, you can always be sure of launching your program with the same entry point regardless of which files are open. For example:

    ```
    "program": "/Users/Me/Projects/PokemonGo-Bot/
    pokemongo_bot/event_handlers/__init__.py",
    ```

- **python:** Full path that points to the Python interpreter to be used for debugging.

  If not determined, this setting defaults to the interpreter identified in the python.pythonPath setting, which is equivalent to using the value ${config:python.pythonPath}. To apply a different interpreter, identify its path instead in the python property of a debug configuration.

As an option, you can also use a custom environment variable that is defined on every platform to contain the full path to the Python interpreter to use, so that no other folder paths are needed. Once you need to pass arguments to the Python interpreter, you can use the pythonArgs property.

- **pythonArgs:** Specifies arguments to pass to the Python interpreter using the syntax "pythonArgs": ["<arg 1>", "<arg 2>"].

- **args:** Specifies arguments to pass to the Python program. Each element of the argument string that is separated by a space have to be contained within quotes, for example:

```
"args": ["--quiet", "--no-repeat", "--port",
"1593"],
```

- **stopOnEntry:** When set to true, breaks the debugger at the first line of the program being debugged. If omitted (by default) or set to false, the debugger runs the program to the first breakpoint.

- **console:** Specifies how program output is presented as long as the defaults for redirectOutput are not edited. Most widely used console values are listed in Table 2-11.

Table 2-11. *Output values*

Value	Where output is displayed
"internalConsole"	VS Code debug console. If redirectOutput is set to False, no output is displayed.
"integratedTerminal"	VS Code Integrated Terminal. If redirectOutput is set to True, output is also displayed in the debug console.
"externalTerminal"	Separate console window. If redirectOutput is set to True, output is also displayed in the debug console.

- **cwd:** Specifies the current working directory for the debugger, which is the basic folder for any relative paths used in code. Once omitted, defaults to ${workspaceFolder} (the folder open in VS Code). As an example, say ${workspaceFolder} contains a py_code folder containing app.py, and a data folder containing salaries.csv. If you start the debugger on py_code/app.py, then the relative paths to the data file vary depending on the value of cwd (Table 2-12).[16]

Table 2-12. *Date file paths*

cwd	Relative path to data file
Omitted or ${workspaceFolder}	data/salaries.csv
${workspaceFolder}/py_code	../data/salaries.csv
${workspaceFolder}/data	salaries.csv

---

[16] Visual Studio Code, "Python Debugging in VS Code."

- **redirectOutput:** When set to true (by default for internalConsole), causes the debugger to print all output from the program into the VS Code debug output window. If set to false (by default for integratedTerminal and externalTerminal), program output is not displayed in the debugger output window. This option is usually disabled when using "console": "integratedTerminal" or "console": "externalTerminal" because there is no need to duplicate the output in the debug console.

- **justMyCode:** When omitted or set to true (by default), restricts debugging to user-written code only. Set to false to also enable debugging of standard library functions.

- **Django:** When set to true, activates debugging features specific to the Django web framework.

- **sudo:** When set to true and used with "console": "externalTerminal", allows for debugging apps that require elevation. Applying an external console is necessary to capture the password.

- **pyramid:** When set to true, makes sure that a Pyramid app is launched with the necessary command-line pserve command.

- **env:** Sets optional environment variables for the debugger process beyond system environment variables, which the debugger always inherits. The values for these variables must be entered as strings.

- **envFile:** Optional path to a file that contains environment variable definitions.

- **gevent:** If set to true, enables debugging of gevent monkey-patched code.

Conditional Breakpoints

Breakpoints can also be set to trigger based on expressions, hit counts, or a combination of both. The Python extension support hit counts that are integers, as well as integers preceded by the ==, >, >=, <, <=, and % operators. For instance, you can set a breakpoint to trigger after five occurrences by setting a hitcount of >5.

Invoking a Breakpoint in Code

In your Python code, you can call debugpy.breakpoint() at any point where you want to pause the debugger during a debugging session.

Breakpoint Validation

The Python extension automatically detects breakpoints that are set on nonexecutable lines, such as pass statements or the middle of a multiline statement. In such cases, running the debugger moves the breakpoint to the nearest valid line to ensure that code execution stops at that point.

Debugging Specific App Types

The configuration dropdown has a variety of different options for general app types (Table 2-13).[17]

---

[17] Visual Studio Code, "Python Debugging in VS Code."

Table 2-13. *Popular configuration descriptions for Python*

Configuration	Description
Attach	See Remote debugging in the previous section.
Django	Specifies "program": "${workspaceFolder}/manage.py", "args": ["runserver"]. Also adds "django": true to enable debugging of Django HTML templates.
Flask	See Flask debugging.
Gevent	Adds "gevent": true to the standard integrated terminal configuration.
Pyramid	Removes program, adds "args": ["${workspaceFolder}/development. ini"], adds "jinja": true for enabling template debugging, and adds "pyramid": true to ensure that the program is launched with the necessary pserve command.
Scrapy	Specifies "module": "scrapy" and adds "args": ["crawl", "specs", "-o", "bikes.json"].
Watson	Specifies "program": "${workspaceFolder}/console.py" and "args": ["dev", "runserver", "--noreload=True"].

Summary

In this chapter we covered several programming basics in VS Code from the perspective of Python developers, such as linting, debugging, and code formatting.

In the next chapter, we will delve deeper into VS Code for Python development and continue with additional code paradigm and tips.

CHAPTER 3

Setting Up the Environment and Testing

VS Code includes multiple handy tools for building and debugging any application. Especially when the Python extension is enabled, VS Code becomes a very convenient, dream-like working environment for Python developers. This chapter discusses Python environments and how to make use of them, how to configure Python project on VS Code to get the most out of it, and how to work with the Jupyter ecosystem, which can be a powerful tool in the hands of a moderately IT-literate user. This chapter also covers how to work with the Jupyter Notebook extension.

Setting Up Your Environment

An environment in Python stands for the surrounding context in which a Python program operates, and consists of an interpreter and many other installed packages of your choice. The Python extension for VS Code provides smooth integration features for working with different environments.

© Sufyan bin Uzayr 2021
S. bin Uzayr, *Optimizing Visual Studio Code for Python Development*,
https://doi.org/10.1007/978-1-4842-7344-9_3

By default, any Python interpreter that you have installed operates in its own global environment, which is not specific to any one project. For instance, if you run python (on Windows) or python3 (on macOS and Linux) at a new command prompt, you are running in that interpreter's global environment. Therefore, any packages that you install or uninstall have an impact on the global environment and all programs that you run within that environment. It is also good to note that the Python extension version 2018.8.1 and all the other versions after that automatically update environments.

Even though administering projects in the global environment is an easy way to get started, that environment will, with time, become cluttered and disarranged with many different packages that have been installed for different projects. Such clutter makes it complicated to thoroughly test an application against a specific set of packages with modular versions, which is exactly the kind of environment you would need to set up on a build server or web server.

Because of that, developers often create a virtual environment for a project. A virtual environment represents a subfolder in a project that has a copy of a specific interpreter. Once you activate the virtual environment, any packages you install are installed only in that environment's subfolder. When you then run a Python program within that environment, you know that it's running against only those specific packages. At the same time, if you are not using a virtual environment, and you have more than one version of Python installed and set in the path variable, you might need to specify the Python interpreter to utilize in the terminal for installing packages to the global environment. While it is possible to open a virtual environment folder as a workspace, it is not highly recommended to do so as it might cause issues with using the Python extension.

Another type of environment that needs to be mentioned is a Conda environment. Conda environment is a virtual environment that is designed and managed using the Conda package manager.

Conda is widely known for creating environments with interrelated dependencies as well as binary sets. Unlike virtual environments, which are created for particular projects, Conda environments are available globally on any given device and for any project. This availability makes it easy to modify several distinct Conda features and then choose the appropriate one for any scoop of work.

As previously mentioned, the Python extension automatically recognizes existing Conda environments provided that the environment has a Python interpreter. To illustrate, the following command creates a Conda environment with the Python 3.4 interpreter and a few libraries, which VS Code then displays in the list of available interpreters:

```
conda create -n env-01 python=3.4 scipy=0.15.0 astroid babel
```

In contrast, if you do not specify an interpreter in a timely manner, as with conda create --name env-00, the environment will simply not appear in the list.

In addition, if you create a new Conda environment while VS Code is running, use the Reload Window command to refresh the environment list shown with Python: Select Interpreter; otherwise, you may not see the environment there. It may take a short time to appear; try waiting 15 seconds before using the command again.

To ensure that the environment is set up right from a shell perspective, one option would be to use an Anaconda prompt with the activated environment to launch VS Code using the code . command. At that point, select the interpreter using the Command Palette or by clicking on the status bar. Even though the Python extension for VS Code does not yet have direct integration with Conda environment.yml files, VS Code itself can act as a great YAML editor. Conda environments cannot be automatically activated in the VS Code Integrated Terminal if the default shell is set to PowerShell. If you want to change the shell, you should check out Integrated terminal Configuration menu.

You can manually determine the path to the Conda executable to use for activation (version 4.4+). In order to do so, open the Command Palette (Ctrl+Shift+P) and enter Preferences: Open User Settings. Then set the appropriate path with python.condaPath, which is in the Python extension section of User Settings.

Manually Specifying an Interpreter

If you see that VS Code does not automatically find an interpreter you need to use, you can set the path to it manually in your Workspace Settings settings.json file. With any of the entries that follow, you can add the line as a sibling to other existing settings. Select the File (Code on macOS) ➤ Preferences ➤ Settings menu command (Ctrl+,) to open your Settings, and select Workspace. Then do any of the following steps:

Create or edit an existing entry for python.pythonPath with the full path to the Python executable (if you edit settings.json directly, add the following line as the setting):

- **For Windows:**

```
"python.pythonPath": "c:/python36/python.exe",
```

- **For macOS and Linux:**

```
"python.pythonPath": "/home/python36/python",
```

You can also use python.pythonPath to indicate a virtual environment, such as:

- **Windows:**

```
"python.pythonPath": "c:/dev/ala/venv/Scripts/
python.exe",
```

- **macOS/Linux:**

```
"python.pythonPath": "/home/abc/dev/ala/venv/bin/
python",
```

You can use an environment variable in the path setting using the syntax ${env:VARIABLE}. For instance, if you have added a variable named PYTHON_INSTALL_LOC with a path to an interpreter, you can then apply the following setting value:

```
"python.pythonPath": "${env:PYTHON_INSTALL_LOC}",
```

At the same time, since variable substitution is only supported in VS Code settings files, it will not work in .env environment files.

By making use of an environment variable, you can easily transfer a project between operating systems where the paths are different. Just make sure you set the environment variable on the operating system first.

To create a virtual environment, write down the following command, where ".venv" is the name of the environment folder:

```
# macOS and Linux
# You might need to run sudo apt-get install python3-venv first
python3 -m venv .venv
```

```
# Windows
# You can also use py -3 -m venv .venv
python -m venv .venv
```

Once you create a new virtual environment, a prompt will be displayed to let you select it for the workspace. If you notice that the active command generates the message "Activate.ps1 is not digitally signed. You cannot run this script on the current system.", then you would have to temporarily change the PowerShell execution policy to allow scripts to run.

Python environment prompt adds the path to the Python interpreter from the new virtual environment to your general workspace settings. That environment will then be applied when installing packages and running code through the Python extension. This will be discussed in detail in Chapter 4, covering Django and the Flask projects.

Selecting and Activating an Environment

By default, the Python extension searches for and uses the first Python interpreter it finds in the system path. If it does not recognize any interpreter, it issues a warning. On macOS, the extension also issues a warning if you are using the OS-installed Python interpreter, because you normally want to use an interpreter you install directly. In both cases, you can disable these warnings by setting python.disableInstallationCheck to true in your user settings.

To select a specific environment, you should use the Python: Select Interpreter command from the Command Palette (Ctrl+Shift+P). You can switch in-between environments at any time; switching environments is also helpful if you need to test different sections of your project with different interpreters or library versions if requested.

The Python: Select Interpreter command comes with a list of available global environments, Conda environments, and virtual environments. It is also important to note that on Windows, it can take a little time for VS Code to detect available Conda environments. During that process, you may see "(cached)" before the path to an environment is ready. The label indicates that VS Code is presently processing with cached information for that environment.

Choosing an interpreter from the list adds an entry for python. pythonPath with the path to the interpreter inside your Workspace Settings. Because the path is part of the workspace settings, the same environment should already be selected at the time you open that workspace. If you would need to set up a default interpreter for your applications, you can instead include an entry for python.pythonPath manually inside your User Settings. To do so, open the Command Palette

(Ctrl+Shift+P) and enter Preferences: Open User Settings. After that, you can set python.pythonPath, which is in the Python extension section of User Settings, with the appropriate interpreter.

The Python extension utilizes the selected environment for running Python code using the Python: Run Python File in Terminal command, providing standard language services such as auto-complete, syntax checking, linting, and formatting when you have a .py file open in the editor, and opening a terminal with the Terminal: Create New Integrated Terminal command. In the latter case, VS Code is expected to automatically activate the selected environment.

Environments and Terminal Windows

After using Python: Select Interpreter, that interpreter is applied when right-clicking a file and selecting Python: Run Python File in Terminal. The environment is also activated automatically any time you use the Terminal: Create New Integrated Terminal command unless you change the python.terminal.activateEnvironment setting to false. Nevertheless, launching VS Code from a shell where a certain Python environment is activated does not automatically activate that environment in the default Integrated Terminal. Use the Terminal: Create New Integrated Terminal command after VS Code is running. Also, Conda environments cannot be automatically operated in the integrated terminal if PowerShell is set as the integrated shell. You should see Integrated terminal - Configuration in order to change the shell.

Any changes you make to an activated environment within the terminal will be permanent. For instance, using Conda install <package> from the terminal with a Conda environment activated installs the package into that environment for good. At the same time, using pip install in a terminal with a virtual environment activated adds the package to that environment.

Changing interpreters with the Python: Select Interpreter command does not cause any difference to terminal panels that are already open. Therefore, you can activate separate environments in a split terminal: simply select the first interpreter, create a terminal for it, select a different interpreter, and then use the split button (Ctrl+Shift+5) in the terminal title bar.

Choosing a Debugging Environment

By default, the python.pythonPath setting determines which Python interpreter to apply for debugging. However, if you have a pythonPath property in the debug configuration of launch.json, that interpreter is applied instead. To be more precise, VS Code uses the following order of precedence when deciding which interpreter to employ for debugging:

1. pythonPath property of the selected debug configuration in launch.json

2. python.pythonPath setting in the workspace settings.json

3. python.pythonPath setting in the user settings.json

The extension automatically searches for interpreters in the given locations:

- Standard install paths such as /usr/local/bin, /usr/ sbin, /sbin, c:\\python27, c:\\python36

- Virtual environments located directly under the workspace (project) folder

- Virtual environments located in the folder identified by the python.venvPath setting, which can contain multiple virtual environments. The extension looks for virtual environments in the first-level subfolders of venvPath

- Virtual environments located in a ~/.virtualenvs folder for virtualenvwrapper

- Interpreters installed by pyenv

- Virtual environments located in the path identified by WORKON_HOME and used by virtualenvwrapper

Conda environments should include a Python interpreter. As a rule, VS Code does not show Conda environments that do not have an interpreter. Interpreters installed in a .direnv folder for direnv under the workspace (or project) folder. You can also manually define an interpreter if VS Code does not locate it automatically.

Environment Variable Definitions File

An environment variable definitions file is an ordinary text file that includes key-value pairs in the form of environment_variable=value, with # applied for comments. Multiline values are not supported, but values can refer to any other environment variable that is already included in the system or earlier in the file. Environment variable definitions files can be applied for scenarios such as debugging and tool execution (including linters, formatters, IntelliSense, and testing tools), but are not applied to the terminal.

By default, the Python extension firstly looks for and loads a file named .env in the current workspace folder, and then applies those definitions. The file is recognized by the default entry "python.envFile": "${workspaceFolder}/.env" in your user General settings. You can modify the python.envFile setting at any time to apply a different definitions file.

A debug configuration has an enviable property that also defaults to the .env file in the current workspace. This function allows you to easily set variables for debugging purposes that replace variables under the default .env file. For instance, when developing a web application, you might want to rapidly switch between development and production servers. Instead of coding the different URLs and other settings into your application directly, you could use separate definitions files for each.

Variable Substitution

When determining an environment variable in a definitions file, you can use the value of any existing environment variable with the following general syntax:

```
<VARIABLE>=...${env:EXISTING_VARIABLE}...
```

where ... stands for any other text as used in the value, and the curly braces are strictly required. In the limits of this syntax, the following rules apply directly:

- Variables are operated in the order they appear in the .env file, so you can use any variable that is included earlier in the file.

- Single or double quotes do not have an effect on the substituted value and are included in the defined value. For instance, if the value of VAR1 is abcedfg, then VAR2='${env:VAR1}' assigns the value 'abcedfg' to VAR2.

- The $ character can be omitted with a backslash, as in \$.

- You can apply recursive substitution, such as PYTHONPATH=${env:PROJ_DIR}:${env:PYTHONPATH} (where PROJ_DIR is any other environment variable).

- You can apply only simple substitution; nesting such as ${_${env:VAR1}_EX} is not supported.

Entries with unsupported syntax are left unmodified.

Using the PYTHONPATH Variable

The PYTHONPATH environment variable identifies additional locations where the Python interpreter should be looking for modules. In VS Code, PYTHONPATH can be set via the terminal settings (such as terminal. integrated.env.*) and within an .env file.

If you are applying the terminal settings, PYTHONPATH starts affecting any tools that are run within the terminal by a user, as well as any action the extension carries out for a user that is completed through the terminal, such as debugging. Yet in this case, when the extension is executing an action that is not routed through the terminal, such as the use of a linter or formatter, then this setting will not have any influence on module outlook.

When PYTHONPATH is set using an .env file, it will affect everything the extension does on your behalf and actions completed by the debugger, but it will not have any affect tools run in the terminal. If necessary, you can set PYTHONPATH using both practices.

A good example of when to use PYTHONPATH would be if you have source code in a src folder and tests in a tests folder. When running tests, however, those tests cannot ordinarily access modules in src unless you hard-code relative paths. In order to prevent this problem, be sure to add the path to src to PYTHONPATH.

The value of PYTHONPATH can hold in multiple locations separated by os.pathsep: a semicolon (;) on Windows and a colon (:) on Linux and macOS. Invalid paths are usually simply disregarded. If you find that your value for PYTHONPATH is not operating as expected, make sure that you are adding the correct separator between locations for the operating system. For instance, adding a colon to separate locations on Windows, or adding a semicolon to separate locations on Linux and macOS, results in an invalid value for PYTHONPATH, which is overlooked. PYTHONPATH does not specify a path to a Python interpreter itself, and should not be used together with the python.pythonPath setting.

The next section describes how to run our Python projects.

Running Your Projects

Start by verifying the Python installation on your machine by running the standard commands:

```
Linux/macOS: python3 --version
Windows: py -3 --version
```

You are now ready to start VS Code in a project (workspace) folder (Figure 3-1).

Figure 3-1. *Running Python projects in VS Code*

Using a command prompt or terminal, set up an empty folder called "hello", navigate into it, and open VS Code in that folder by entering the following commands:

```
mkdir hello
cd hello
code
```

At this point, make sure you are using an Anaconda command prompt. By starting VS Code in a folder, that folder becomes your workspace. VS Code stores settings that belong to that particular workspace in .vscode/settings.json, which are separate from user settings that are stored globally. Alternately, you can run VS Code through the operating system User Interface by accessing File ➤ Open Folder to open the project folder.

Selecting a Python Interpreter

Python by default is an interpreted language, and in order to run Python code and get Python IntelliSense, you must specify to VS Code which interpreter to apply.

From within VS Code, choose a Python 3 interpreter by opening the Command Palette (Ctrl+Shift+P), and then start typing the Python: Select Interpreter command to search; after that, select the command. You can also use the Select Python Environment function on the Status Bar if available (it may already display information on a selected interpreter).

The command presents options of available interpreters that VS Code can find automatically, including virtual environments. If you do not see the interpreter you are looking for, trying searching at Configuring Python environments. You should also note that when using an Anaconda distribution, the correct interpreter will normally have the suffix ('base':conda): for example, Python 3.7.3 64-bit ('base':conda).

Opting for an interpreter sets the python.pythonPath value in your workspace settings to the path of the interpreter. To see that setting, select File ➤ Preferences ➤ Settings (Code ➤ Preferences ➤ Settings for macOS), then click on the Workspace Settings tab. At the same time, if you select an interpreter without a workspace folder open, VS Code sets python.pythonPath in your user settings instead, which activates the default interpreter for VS Code in general. The user setting enables you to always have a default interpreter for Python projects. In other words, the workspace settings lets you override the user setting.

Creating a Python Hello World Source Code File

From the File Explorer toolbar, select the New File button on the hello folder. Name the file hello.py, and it automatically opens in the editor: File Explorer hello.py. By using the .py file extension, you let VS Code interpret this file as a Python program, so that it reads the contents with the Python extension and the interpreter of your choice. The same File Explorer toolbar also allows you to make folders within your workspace to help you order and organize your code. For that you can use the New folder button to effortlessly create a folder.

After you have set a code file in your Workspace, enter the following source code in hello.py:

```
msg = "Hello World"
print(msg)
```

When you start typing, you should be able to observe how IntelliSense presents auto-completion options. IntelliSense and auto-completion operate for standard Python modules as well as for other packages you have installed into the environment of the selected Python interpreter. It also offers completions for methods available on object types. For instance, because the msg variable contains a string, IntelliSense provides string methods for you to type them.

IntelliSense also appears for a variable whose type provides methods. You can freely experiment with IntelliSense and try more functions, but it is always advised to then revert your changes so you have only the msg variable and the print call, and save the file (Ctrl+S).

Running Hello World

It is quite simple to run hello.py with Python: click the Run Python File in Terminal play button in the top-right side of the editor. The button accesses a terminal panel in which your Python interpreter is automatically activated, then starts running python3 hello.py (macOS and Linux) or python hello.py (Windows).

There are three other options for running Python code within VS Code:

- Right-click anywhere in the editor window and select Run Python File in Terminal (which saves the file automatically).

- Run Python File in Terminal command in the Python editor. You should select one or more lines, then press Shift+Enter or right-click and select Run Selection/Line in Python Terminal. This command is suitable for testing separate sections of a file.

- Use the Command Palette (Ctrl+Shift+P). Select the Python: Start REPL command to open a REPL terminal for the currently selected Python interpreter. In the REPL, you should then enter and run lines of code one by one.

Running the Python Debugger

The procedure to run the debugging process for the Hello World program is also quite straightforward. You'll first need to configure and initialize it, and then define the variables. The next two sections explain how.

Configuring and Initializing the Debugger

Set a breakpoint on line 2 of hello.py by placing the cursor on the print call and clicking F9. As an alternative, you can click in the editor's left gutter, next to the line numbers; once you set a breakpoint, a red circle appears in the gutter.

Next, in order to initialize the debugger, press F5. Since this is your first time debugging this file, a configuration menu will open from the Command Palette, letting you select the type of debug configuration you would like to run for the active file. It is important to know that VS Code uses JSON files for all of its various configurations; launch.json is the standard name for a file that has debugging configurations.

These different configuration methods are fully explained in Debugging configurations. If you are new to this procedure, select Python File, which is the configuration that runs the current file shown in the editor using the currently selected Python interpreter. The debugger will stop at the first line of the file breakpoint. The current line is identified with a yellow arrow in the left margin. If you examine the Local variables window at this point, you can see how defined msg variable showing in the Local pane.

Defining Variables

A debug toolbar appears along the top with the following commands from left to right: continue (F5), step over (F10), step into (F11), step out (Shift+F11), restart (Ctrl+Shift+F5), and stop (Shift+F5).

The Status Bar can also change color (orange for most of the themes) to show that you are in debug mode. The Python Debug Console also comes out automatically in the lower right panel to show the commands being run, along with the program output. To continue running the program, select the continue command on the debug toolbar (F5) and the debugger will run the program to the end.

Installing and Using Packages

This section explains how to run packages. In Python, packages let you obtain a number of useful code libraries, typically from PyPI. For this example, we shall try using the matplotlib and NumPy packages to make up a graphical plot, as is commonly done with data science.

A best practice among Python developers is to refrain from installing packages into a global interpreter environment. Instead, you should use a project-specific virtual environment that has a copy of a global interpreter. When you activate that environment, any packages you then install are separated from other environments. Such isolation prevents many complications that can occur from conflicting package versions. In order to create a virtual environment and install the required packages, enter the following commands as appropriate for your operating system:

- **For Windows:**

```
py -3 -m venv .venv
.venv\scripts\activate
```

  If the activate command generates the message "Activate.ps1 is not digitally signed. You cannot run this script on the current system.", then you need to temporarily change the PowerShell execution policy to allow scripts to run.

- **For macOS and Linux:**

```
python3 -m venv .venv
source .venv/bin/activate
```

  You can select your new environment by using the Python: Select Interpreter command from the Command Palette. But when you create a new virtual environment, you should be prompted by VS Code to set it as the default for your workspace folder. Once chosen, the environment will automatically be activated when you access a new terminal.

When installing the packages try not to use it with Anaconda distributions, because they include matplotlib already:

- **For macOS:**

```
python3 -m pip install matplotlib
```

- **For Windows (might require additional elevation):**

```
python -m pip install matplotlib

# Linux (Debian) (you might need to run as sudo)
apt-get install python3-tk
python3 -m pip install matplotlib
```

When you rerun the program (with or without the debugger) a few moments later, a plot window should appear with the output: matplotlib output

Once you are finished, do not forget to type deactivate in the terminal window to deactivate the virtual environment.

Now, we will turn our attention to the Jupyter Notebook and its usage in VS Code.

Supportting Jupyter

Jupyter Notebook enables creating and sharing files that contain live code, equations, text, and visualizations, and is considered to be one of the greatest tools for data science because of its simplicity and interactivity (Figure 3-2).

Figure 3-2. *Jupyter Notebook with Python in Visual Studio Code*

Jupyter Notebooks are also used with other programming languages in addition to Python, such as R, Julia, and Scala. To enable the same rich Jupyter Notebook experience for other languages, the Jupyter support has been refactored out of the Python extension and into the Jupyter extension. This way it is much easier to build new Jupyter experiences for languages beyond Python by establishing a dependency on the Jupyter extension, which itself has no dependency on the Python runtime or the Python extension.

The Jupyter extension provides basic notebook support for any language kernel that is supported in Jupyter Notebooks today. Most language kernels will operate Jupyter without any need for modification. However, to enable advanced features such as full IntelliSense and debugging, there might be modifications needed in the VS Code language extensions.

Jupyter (also formerly known as IPython Notebook) is an open-source project that enables you to easily combine Markdown text and executable Python source code on one platform called a notebook. VS Code supports working with Jupyter Notebooks by default, as well as through Python code files. This section will cover the support offered through Python code files and illustrate how to work with Jupyter-like code cells, run code in the Python Interactive Window, inspect and filter variables using the Variable explorer and data viewer, and debug and export a Jupyter Notebook. In order to work with Jupyter Notebooks, you must first activate an Anaconda environment in VS Code or another Python environment in which you have installed the Jupyter package. To select an environment, use the Python: Select Interpreter command from the Command Palette (Ctrl+Shift+P).

Once the appropriate environment is activated, you can freely design and run Jupyter-like code cells, connect to a remote Jupyter server for running code cells, and export Python files as Jupyter Notebooks.

Jupyter Code Cells

You define Jupyter-like code cells within Python code using a # %% comment:

```
# %%
msg = "Hello World"
print(msg)

# %%
msg = "Hello again"
print(msg)
```

Make sure you save the preceding code in a file with a .py extension.

Selecting a command starts Jupyter, then runs the appropriate cell(s) in the Python Interactive window. It is also possible to run code cells using (Ctrl+Enter) or the Python: Run Selection/Line in Python Terminal command (Shift+Enter). After writing down this command, the Python extension automatically moves the cursor to the next cell. If you are in the last cell in the file, the extension automatically inserts another # %% delimiter for a new cell, mimicking the behavior of a Jupyter Notebook.

You can also click in the margin to the left of line numbers to set breakpoints. Then you can use Debug Cell to refresh a debugging session for that code cell. The debugger stops execution at breakpoints and lets you step through code one line at a time and inspect variables.

Additional Commands and Keyboard Shortcuts

Table 3-1 presents a few additional commands and keyboard shortcuts supported when working with code cells.[1]

Table 3-1. *Additional commands and shortcuts*

Command	Keyboard shortcut
Python: Go to Next Cell	Ctrl+Alt+]
Python: Go to Previous Cell	Ctrl+Alt+[
Python: Extend Selection by Cell Above	Ctrl+Shift+Alt+[
Python: Extend Selection by Cell Below	Ctrl+Shift+Alt+]
Python: Move Selected Cells Up	Ctrl+; U
Python: Move Selected Cells Down	Ctrl+; D
Python: Insert Cell Above	Ctrl+; A
Python: Insert Cell Below	Ctrl+; B
Python: Insert Cell Below Position	Ctrl+; S
Python: Delete Selected Cells	Ctrl+; X
Python: Change Cell to Code	Ctrl+; C
Python: Change Cell to Markdown	Ctrl+; M

---

[1] Visual Studio Code, "Python Interactive Window," https://code.visualstudio.com/docs/python/jupyter-support-py, accessed July 29, 2021.

Python Interactive Window

The Python Interactive window can be used as a fully functioning console with arbitrary code (with or without code cells). To employ the window as a console, you have to open it with the Jupyter: create Interactive Window command from the Command Palette, then type in code, using Enter to go to a new line and Shift+Enter to run the code. To use the window with a file, you can also apply the Jupyter, simply by Running Current File in Python Interactive Window command from the Command Palette.

Plot Viewer

The Python Interactive window has full IntelliSense that includes code completions, member lists, quick info for methods, and parameter hints. These features allow you to be just as productive typing in the Python Interactive window as you are in the code editor.

The Plot Viewer gives you the ability to work more deeply with the plots inside the IntelliSense. In the viewer, you can pan, zoom, and navigate plots in the currently ongoing session. You can also export plots to PDF, SVG, and PNG formats.

Within the Python Interactive window, double-click any plot to open it in the viewer, or select the expand button on the upper left corner of the plot. However, the Python Interactive window supports rendering plots only created with matplotlib and Altair.

Live Share for Python Interactive

The Python Interactive window also supports Visual Studio Live Share for real-time collaboration. Live Share offers you options to co-edit and co-debug while sharing audio, servers, terminals, diffs, comments, and more. This characteristic, however, requires the Live Share extensions to be installed on both host and guest machines.

Variable Explorer and Data Viewer

Within the Python Interactive window it is possible to view, inspect, and filter the variables within your current Jupyter session. By expanding the Variables section after running code and cells, you can look through a list of the current variables, which will be automatically updated as variables are used in code.

For more information about your variables, you can double-click on a row or use the Show variable in the data viewer setting to see a more detailed view of a variable in the Data Viewer. Once open, you can review the values by looking over the rows. Variable explorer is enabled by default but can be easily turned off in settings via Python ➤ Data Science: Show Jupyter Variable Explorer.

Connecting to a Remote Jupyter Server

You can transfer intensive computation in a Jupyter Notebook to other computers by simply connecting to a remote Jupyter server. When connected, code cells run on the remote server rather than the local computer.

To connect to a remote Jupyter server, run the Jupyter: Specify local or remote Jupyter server for connections command from the Command Palette (Ctrl+Shift+P), and afterward make a choice how you would like to connect to a Jupyter server.

If working remotely, provide the server's URI (hostname) with the authentication token included with a ?token= URL parameter when prompted. If you start the server in the VS Code terminal with an authentication token enabled, the URL with the token typically shows in the terminal output from where you should copy it. At the same time, you should specify a username and password after providing the URI.

The Python Interactive window designates where code is run by displaying the URI. For better security, Microsoft recommends configuring your Jupyter server with security precautions such as SSL and token support. This will assist and ensure that requests sent to the Jupyter server are authenticated and links to the remoter server are safely encrypted.

Converting Jupyter Notebooks to Python Code File

When you have activated an environment with Jupyter installed, you can open a Jupyter Notebook file (.ipynb) in VS Code and then convert it to Python code. Once you've complete the conversion, you can run the code as you would usually do with any other Python file, and also use the VS Code debugger. Opening and debugging notebooks in VS Code is an easy way to find and resolve code bugs, which is rather inconvenient to do directly in a Jupyter Notebook.

Every time you open a notebook file, VS Code will open it in the Notebook Editor automatically. You can use the convert icon on the toolbar to convert the Notebook (.ipynb) file to a Python file (.py). Be sure to select the convert icon followed by "Python Script", wait a few seconds, and then VS Code opens the converted notebook as an untitled file. The notebook's cells are delimited in the Python file with # %% comments; markdown cells are converted wholly to comments preceded with # %% [markdown], and rendered as HTML in the interactive window along with the code and other output such as graphs and tables. The first time you run code cells in a Python file, the Python extension starts a Jupyter server. It usually takes some time for the server to pick up and for the Python Interactive window to show the results of the code.

Debugging a Jupyter Notebook

The VS Code debugger lets you analyze your code, set breakpoints, examine its state, and scan for problems. Using the debugger is a fast way to look for and correct errors in notebook code.

In VS Code, activate a Python environment in which Jupyter is installed, as described at the beginning of this chapter. Import the notebook's .ipynb file into VS Code and start the debugger using one of the following options:

- For the whole notebook, open the Command Palette (Ctrl+Shift+P) and run the Jupyter: Debug Current File in the Python Interactive Window command.

- For an individual cell, apply the Debug Cell function that appears above the cell. The debugger specifically starts on the code in that cell. By default, Debug Cell just steps into user code. If you need to step into nonuser code, you will have to uncheck Data Science: Debug Just My Code in the Python extension settings (Ctrl+,).

- Make sure you familiarize yourself with the general debugging features of VS Code, such as inspecting variables, setting breakpoints, and other activities

If any issues occur during the process, stop the debugger, correct your code, save the file, and start the debugger again. When you are satisfied with your code, save the file and then export the notebook. You can then upload the notebook to your normal Jupyter environment.

Exporting a Jupyter Notebook

In addition to accessing a Jupyter Notebook, you can also apply one of the following commands from the Command Palette (Ctrl+Shift+P) to export content from a Python file in VS Code to a Jupyter Notebook (with the .ipynb extension).

- **Jupyter:** Export Current Python File as Jupyter Notebook: creates a Jupyter Notebook from the contents of the current file, using the # %% and # %% [markdown] delimiters to specify their respective cell types.

- **Jupyter:** Export Current Python File and Output as Jupyter Notebook: create a Jupyter Notebook from the contents of the current file and includes output from code cells.

- **Jupyter:** Export Interactive Window as Jupyter Notebook: creates a Jupyter Notebook from the contents of the Python Interactive window.

After exporting the contents, VS Code displays a prompt through which you can open the notebook in a browser. Jupyter stores different data (such as configuration, runtime) in a number of different locations. Environment variables may be set to customize for the location of each file type. Jupyter keeps data files (nbextensions, kernelspecs) separately from runtime files (logs, pid files, connection files) and from configuration (config files, custom.js).

Configuration Files

Config files are stored by default in the ~/.jupyter directory. JUPYTER_CONFIG_DIR is used for for config file location and JUPYTER_CONFIG_PATH is used for config file locations.

JUPYTER_CONFIG_DIR

You should set this environment variable to use a particular directory, other than the default, for Jupyter config files. Besides the JUPYTER_CONFIG_DIR, additional directories to select can be specified through JUPYTER_CONFIG_PATH.

JUPYTER_CONFIG_PATH

You can set this environment variable to provide extra directories for the config search path.

:envvar:`JUPYTER_CONFIG_PATH` should contain a series of directories, separated by

`` os.pathsep`` (``;`` on Windows, ``:`` on Unix). For example, JUPYTER_CONFIG_PATH can be placed if notebook or server extensions are installed in a custom prefix. Because notebook and server extensions are automatically enabled through configuration files, automatic enabling will only work if the custom prefix's etc/jupyter directory is included to the Jupyter config search path.

Besides the user config directory, Jupyter has a search path of extra locations from which a config file will be loaded. Following is a list of the locations to be searched, in order of relevance:

- **For Unix:**

```
JUPYTER_CONFIG_DIR
JUPYTER_CONFIG_PATH
{sys.prefix}/etc/jupyter/
/usr/local/etc/jupyter/ /etc/jupyter/
```

- **For Windows:**

```
%PROGRAMDATA%\jupyter\
```

To list the config directories currently being used, you can activate this command from the command line:

```
jupyter -paths;
```

The following command will display the config directory specifically:

```
jupyter --config-dir.
```

Data Files

Jupyter utilizes a search path to look for installable data files, such as kernel specs and notebook extensions. When searching for a resource, the code will review the search path starting at the first directory until it finds where the resource is contained. Each category of file is in a subdirectory of each directory of the search path. For instance, kernel specs are placed in kernels subdirectories.

JUPYTER_PATH is used for datafile directory locations and JUPYTER_DATA_DIR is used for data file location.

JUPYTER_PATH

You can set this environment variable to provide extra directories for the data search path. JUPYTER_PATH should restrain a series of directories, separated by os.pathsep (; on Windows, : on Unix). Directories scripted in JUPYTER_PATH are searched before other locations. This is used in addition to other entries, rather than in their replacement:

- **For Linux (and other free desktops):**

```
JUPYTER_DATA_DIR or (if not set) ~/.local/
share/jupyter/ (respects $XDG_DATA_HOME)
{sys.prefix}/share/jupyter/
/usr/local/share/jupyter /usr/share/jupyter
```

- **For Mac:**

  ```
  JUPYTER_DATA_DIR or (if not set) ~/Library/
  Jupyter
  ```

- **For Windows:**

  ```
  JUPYTER_DATA_DIR or (if not set) %APPDATA%\
  jupyter
  %PROGRAMDATA\jupyter
  ```

The config directory for Jupyter data files hold nontransient, nonconfiguration files. Examples include kernelspecs, nbextensions, or templates.

JUPYTER_DATA_DIR

You should set this environment variable to use a particular directory, other than the default, as the user data directory. As mentioned, to list the config directories currently being used, you can run the following command from the command line: jupyter –paths; and jupyter --data-dir shows the data directory specifically.

Runtime File

Items such as connection files, which are only applied for the lifetime of a particular process, have a runtime directory. JUPYTER_RUNTIME_DIR is used for runtime file location.

On Linux and other free desktop platforms, these runtime files are located in $XDG_RUNTIME_DIR/jupyter by default. On other platforms, it's a runtime/subdirectory of the user's data directory. Any other environment variable can also be used to set the runtime directory.

JUPYTER_RUNTIME_DIR

You may set this to override where Jupyter stores runtime files. As mentioned, to list the config directories currently being used, you can use the command jupyter –paths, and jupyter --runtime-dir shows the runtime directory specifically.

Summary

Jupyter Notebook is the most user-friendly, convenient, resourceful, and stable interactive computing environment currently available. It greatly combines rich text cells such as markdown, LaTeX and raw HTML, code cells, and rich, high-value data that contains the computation results. The output can be anything a web page can display, from ordinary text to dynamic visualizations. For this reason, it would be better to run and keep it clear to read as a research file.

Normally, a user should be able to open a notebook in JupyterHub from a link on a GitHub repo, open a notebook from a link received by email, give access to a notebook by storing it on a GitHub repo, give access to a notebook via a cryptic URL, and access to network drives to read or write data without any hassle. The following three methods to share notebooks are most practiced at the moment:

- Sharing via Git

- Sharing viva NFS

- Sharing via Docker NetApp plugin

We have covered a good deal about Jupyter Notebook. In the next chapter, we will turn our attention to Python frameworks such as Django and Flask.

CHAPTER 4

Working with Python Frameworks

In the previous chapter, we covered some core concepts pertaining to Jupyter Notebook. In this chapter we will turn our attention to Python frameworks. Because Python web development has been around for quite a while now, Avarious handy Python frameworks were created to make the life of an ordinary developer much easier. That is exactly how we would describe Python for web development.

Python is known as a very readable, object-oriented programming language. Due to its unique syntax, it is much faster to learn and use its basic features compared to other programming languages such as Java or even C++. The Python framework provides a structure to help users create the apps without having to build every single item from the beginning. In this chapter we'll quickly review Python frameworks ecosystem, create simple codes in VS Code with Django and Flask frameworks, and then explore some basic data science scenarios in VS Code.

© Sufyan bin Uzayr 2021
S. bin Uzayr, *Optimizing Visual Studio Code for Python Development*,
https://doi.org/10.1007/978-1-4842-7344-9_4

Python Frameworks Ecosystem at a Glance

A framework acts as an arrangement designed to support the development of web applications and web APIs. It provides a standard way to build apps while automating the overhead associated with common activities performed in web development. It comes with many reusable characteristics and has two main purposes: simplifying the process of creating web apps, and aiming for the best possible results and saving your time. Python frameworks are also very useful for a number of reasons:

- They cover basic things such as creating autoload files, session files, and index files.

- They provide better functionality to process requests.

- They follow the latest patterns.

- They let you attach necessary third-party resources.

There are many web application frameworks out there, and it might get confusing and challenging to decide which one is the right one for you. When selecting the Python web framework of your choice, there are several things to consider. First, you should take a look at the complexity of your project. If you are working on a smaller application, you should consider applying microframework. If, on the other hand, you are creating a large app project that has all kinds of features and requirements, you might opt for a full-stack framework. In other words, the decision should come from your understanding of the final outcome and the tasks you want to untangle. Another thing to remember is the fact that sometimes a web application framework can stand in the way of web development due to the fact that every framework usually has certain limitations. You can either find your ways of working with them or discard the framework entirely instead of having to go through it.

A web framework is the result of what developers have learned over the past years while programming sites and applications for the web. Frameworks make it easier to reapply code for common HTTP procedures and to structure projects so other developers can effortlessly rebuild and maintain the application. Web frameworks are a concept implemented by Django, Flask, Bottle, Pyramid, Morepath, TurboGears, and several other libraries. Frameworks provide functionality in their code or through extensions to activate operations required to run web applications. These funding operations include:

- URL routing

- Input form handling and validation

- HTML, XML, JSON, and other output formats

- Database connection configuration and data manipulation through an object-relational mapper (ORM)

- Web security against Cross-site request forgery (CSRF), SQL Injection, Cross-site Scripting (XSS)

- Session storage and retrieval

It is also good to keep in mind that not all web frameworks include code for all of this functionality. Frameworks are usually placed on the spectrum from executing a single function to providing every known web framework characteristic.

Whether or not you need to use a web framework in your project at all solely depends on your experience with web development and which project you are running. If you are a beginner programmer and just need to complete a web application as a learning project, then a framework can assist in the understanding of the preceding concepts, such as URL routing, data manipulation, and authentication, that are common tasks for the majority of web applications. On the other hand, if you already have significant web development experience, you may feel like minimal caliber frameworks do not match your project's requirements. In that case, you can experiment with open-source libraries such as Werkzeug for WSGI plumbing with your own code to create your own framework. Although there are plenty of different items in the Python ecosystem to satisfy the needs of web developers, such as Pyramid and Bottle, this chapter focuses on Django and Flask, the two most common and versatile Python frameworks.

Django Development

Django is a high-level Python framework developed for fast, secure, and stable web development (Figure 4-1). Django also has rich support for URL routing, page templates, and working with data.

Figure 4-1. *Django, a popular Python framework*

In this section we shall cover how to work with Django in the VS Code terminal, editor, and debugger.

Installation

You start by making sure you have the latest version of VS Code installed. To successfully complete this Django tutorial, you must install a version of Python 3 in one of the following ways:

- **For all operating systems:** a download from python. org; typically use the Download Python 3.9.1 button that appears first on the page.

- **For Linux:** the built-in Python 3 installation works well, but to download other Python packages you must run sudo apt install python3-pip in the terminal.

- **For macOS:** an installation through Homebrew on macOS using brew install python3.

In addition, no matter which operating systems you use, be sure you download from Anaconda distribution for data science purposes. On Windows, the location of your Python interpreter has to be included in your PATH environment variable. You can check the location by running path at the command prompt. If the Python interpreter's folder is not added, open Windows Settings, search for "environment", select Edit environment variables for your account, and then edit the Path variable to include that folder.

After you are finished with that step, you can install the following (free) extensions:

- **Python (published by Microsoft):** for full Python language support.

- **Django Template:** for template file source highlighting.

- **Django Snippets:** for common Django code. Alternatively, install Djaniero-Django Snippets if you prefer.

Do not forget to reload VS Code after extension installation.

Creating a Project Environment for the Django Tutorial

Creating a virtual environment in which Django is installed is an important step. Using a virtual environment avoids installing Django into a global Python environment and gives you exact control over the libraries engaged in an application. A virtual environment also makes it easy to cover requirements.txt file for the environment.

Begin by creating a project folder for this tutorial, such as hello_django on your file system. In that folder, use the following command (as suitable to your computer) to design a virtual environment named env based on your current interpreter:

- **For Linux:** python3 -m venv env

- **For macOS:** python3 -m venv env

- **For Windows:** python -m venv env

Be sure to use a stock Python installation when activating these commands. If you apply python.exe from an Anaconda installation, you get an error because the ensurepip module is not available, and the environment is left in an incomplete condition.

Next, open the project folder in VS Code by running code or by running VS Code and using the File ➤ Open Folder command. In VS Code, open the Command Palette via View ➤ Command Palette or Ctrl+Shift+P, then select the Python: Select Interpreter command: Django tutorial: opening the Command Palette in VS Code. The command will call a list of available interpreters that VS Code can locate automatically (and your list will vary). From the list, go for the virtual environment in your project folder that starts with ./env or .\env.

You can also create New Integrated Terminal (Ctrl+Shift+`) from the Command Palette, which produces a terminal and automatically activates the virtual environment by running its activation script. On Windows, if your default terminal type is PowerShell, you may get an error that it cannot run activate.ps1 because running scripts is disabled on the system. The error shall also provide a link for information on how to allow scripts. You can also use Terminal: Select Default Shell to set "Command Prompt" or "Git Bash" as your default.

The selected environment should pop up on the left side of the VS Code status bar; notice that the "(venv)" indicator that tells you that you are currently using a virtual environment. In addition, you can modify your environment via the following commands:

- **Update pip in the virtual environment:** python -m pip install --upgrade pip

- **Install Django in the virtual environment:** python -m pip install Django

VS Code activates the environment automatically when you use Terminal: Create New Integrated Terminal (Ctrl+Shift+`). When you open a separate command prompt or terminal, activate the environment by running source env/bin/activate (Linux/macOS) or env\Scripts\Activate.ps1 (Windows). You know the environment is active when the command prompt shows (env) at the beginning. You now have a self-evolved environment ready for writing Django code.

Creating and Running a Minimal Django App

In Django terminology, a Django project is made up of several site-level configuration files together with one or more apps that you employ to a web host to make a full web application. A Django project can produce multiple apps, each of which will normally have an independent function in the project, and the same app can be in various Django projects. In this instance, an app is just a Python package that has certain functions that Django expects.

To create a minimal Django application, it is necessary to first design the basic Django project to serve as the container for the app, and then go on to creating the app itself. For both processes you should apply the Django administrative utility or Django-admin, which is installed together with the Django package.

Creating the Django Project

In the VS Code Terminal where your virtual environment is operating, insert the following command:

```
Django-admin startproject web_project.
```

This startup command assumes (by use of . at the end) that the current folder is your project folder, and creates manage.py within it, which stands for the Django command-line administrative utility for the project. You run administrative commands for the project using python manage. py <command>. As a subfolder you also have a file named web_project, which contains the following files:

- **__init__.py:** an empty file that informs Python that this folder is a Python package.

- **asgi.py:** an entry point for ASGI-compatible web servers to serve your project. You should leave this file as-is to secure the hooks for production web servers.

- **settings.py:** contains settings for Django project, which you modify in the course of developing a web app.

- **urls.py:** contains a table of contents for the Django project, which you can edit in the course of development.

- **wsgi.py:** an entry point for WSGI-compatible web servers to serve your project. It is recommended to leave this file as-is as to provide the hooks for production web servers.

You should also create an empty development database by running the following command: python manage.py migrate. When you run the server for the first time, it generates a default SQLite database in the file DB.sqlite3 that is considered necessary for development purposes but can also be used in production for low-volume web apps. To verify the Django project, make sure your virtual environment is running error-free, then start Django's development server using the command python manage. py runserver. Django's built-in web server is designed only for local development purposes. When you add a web host, however, Django will use the host's web server instead. The wsgi.py and asgi.py modules in the Django project are responsible for getting into the production servers.

If you want to use a different port than the default 8000, you should insert the port number on the command line, such as python manage. py runserver 5000. Ctrl+click the `http://127.0.0.1:8000/` URL in the terminal output window to open your default browser to that address. If Django is installed correctly and the project is still active, you will be able to see the default page shown below. The VS Code terminal output window also presents the server log. Once you are finished, close the browser window and stop the server in VS Code using Ctrl+C in the terminal output window.

Creating a Django App

In the VS Code Terminal where your virtual environment is located, run the administrative utility's start command in your project folder (where manage.py added): python manage.py startapp helloworld. This command will create a folder called helloworld that has a number of code files and one subfolder. With this, you most frequently might work with views.py (that functions as page definition of your web app) and models.py (that has classes defining your data objects). The migrations folder is utilized by Django's administrative utility to administer database versions, as will be discussed later in this chapter. In the same folder, we can also see the files apps.py (for app configuration), admin.py (for creating an administrative interface), and tests.py (for creating tests).

You can modify helloworld/views.py to match the following code and create a single view for the app's home page with the following: from Django.http import HttpResponse

```
def home(request):

 return HttpResponse("Hello, Django!")
```

With that, create a file hello/urls.py with the contents below. The urls.py file is where you identify patterns to route different URLs to their appropriate views. The following code contains one route to map the root URL of the app ("") to the views.home function that you just added to hello/views.py:[1]

```
from django.urls import path
from hello import views
urlpatterns = [
    path("", views.home, name="home"),
]
```

The web_project folder also has a urls.py file, which is where URL routing is actually located. Open web_project/urls.py and edit it to match the following code. This code pulls in the app's hello/urls.py using Django. URLs.include, which keeps the app's routes framed within the app. This procedure is used when a project has not one but multiple apps. In the end, be sure to save all modified files with Ctrl+K S.

---

[1] Visual Studio Code, "Django Tutorial in Visual Studio Code," https://code. visualstudio.com/docs/python/tutorial-django, accessed July 29, 2021.

Creating a Debugger Launch Profile

Fortunately, there is an easier way to run the server and test the app without typing python manage.py runserver every time. It is possible to create a customized launch profile in VS Code, which is also applied for the inevitable exercise of debugging.

First, switch to Run view in VS Code (using the left-side activity bar or F5). You might get the message "To customize Run and Debug create a launch.json file." This means that you do not yet have a launch.json file with debug configurations. VS Code can create that for you once you click on the create a launch.json file link.

Select the launch.json link, and VS Code will start a debug configuration. Select Django from the dropdown and VS Code will include a new launch.json file to a Django run configuration. The launch.json file has a number of different debugging configurations, each of which is a distinct JSON object within the configuration variety.

After that, scroll down to examine the configuration with the name "Python: Django" by scripting:[2]

```
{
    "name": "Python: Django",
    "type": "python",
    "request": "launch",
    "program": "${workspaceFolder}/manage.py",
    "args": [
        "runserver",
    ],
    "django": true
},
```

---

[2] Visual Studio Code, "Django Tutorial in Visual Studio Code."

This configuration makes VS Code run "${workspaceFolder}/manage. py" together with the selected Python interpreter and the arguments in the args list. Launching the VS Code debugger with this configuration would have the same effect as running python manage.py runserver in the VS Code Terminal with your activated virtual environment. The "Django": true entry also allows VS Code to enable debugging of Django page templates.

You can test the configuration any time by selecting the Run ➤ Start Debugging menu command, or clicking on the green Start Debugging arrow next to the list (F5). You should then do Ctrl+click the http://127.0.0.1:8000/ URL in the terminal output window to open the browser and check once again that the app is running properly.

When you are finished, close the browser and stop the debugger. In order to stop the debugger, use the Stop toolbar button (the red square) or the Run ➤ Stop Debugging command (Shift+F5). You can also follow the Run ➤ Start Debugging at any time to test the app, which also has the advantage of automatically saving all modified files.

Exploring the Debugger

Debugging gives you a chance to pause a running program on a specified line of code. When a program is paused you can check out variables, run code in the Debug Console panel, and take advantage of modified files before the debugging session begins.

Before you start, make sure you have stopped the running app at the end of the last session by using Ctrl+C in the terminal. If you leave the app running in one terminal, it continues to use the port. Because of that, when you run the app in the debugger using the same port, the original running app takes all the requests and you will not observe any activity in the app being debugged, and the program will not stop at breakpoints. To put it simply, if the debugger does not seem to be activated, make sure that no other part of the app is still running.

Start with add a route to the urlpatterns list: path("helloworld/<name>" in helloworld/urls.py. The first argument to path defines a route "hello/" that includes a variable string called name. The string is passed to the views.hello_world function specified in the second part of the argument.

Because URL routes are very case-sensitive, if you need the same view function to manage both, you have to define paths for each variant. The name variable defined in the URL route is given as an argument to the hello_there function. As a side note, you should always filter arbitrary user-provided information to prevent various attacks on your app from happening. In this case, the code filters the name argument to include only letters, which avoids injection of control characters, HTML, and others.

You can set a breakpoint at the first line of code in the hello_world function (now = DateTime.now()) by doing any one of the following:

- Press F9 with the cursor on that line

- Select the Run ➤ Toggle Breakpoint menu command

- Click directly in the margin to the left of the line number

The breakpoint appears as a red dot in the left margin. Start the debugger by selecting the Run ➤ Start Debugging menu command, or selecting the green Start Debugging arrow next to the list (F5). A debugging toolbar also pops in VS Code containing commands in the following order: Pause (or Continue, F5), Step Over (F10), Step Into (F11), Step Out (Shift+F11), Restart (Ctrl+Shift+F5), and Stop (Shift+F5). Command output appears in a Python Debug Console terminal. You should open a browser and navigate to http://127.0.0.1:8000/helloworld/VSCode. Before the page loads, VS Code pauses the program at the breakpoint you set. The small yellow arrow on the breakpoint shows that it is the next line of code to run. Use Step Over to run the now = DateTime.now() statement.

On the left side of the VS Code window, you can see a Variables list that shows local variables and arguments. Below that would be listed for Watch, Call Stack, and Breakpoints. In the Locals section, try expanding different values and modifying them with double-clicks (or F2). Changing variables, however, can break the program. Developers usually make changes only to correct values when the code did not produce the right value in the beginning.

When a program is paused, the Debug Console panel allows you to experiment with expressions and try out different parts of code using the current state of the program. For instance, once you have stepped over the line now = DateTime.now(), you might try with different date/time formats. In the editor, choose the code that reads now.strftime("%A, %d %B, %Y at %X"), and then right-click and select Debug: Evaluate to send that code to the debug console, where it shows:

```
now.strftime("%A, %d %B, %Y at %X")
'Friday, 07 June, 2021 at 12:43:32'
```

At the same time, the Debug Console also has exceptions from within the app that may not show in the terminal. For example, if you see a "Paused on exception" message in the Call Stack area of Run view, switch to the Debug Console to see the exception message. To make it easier to repeatedly go to a specific URL such as http://127.0.0.1:8000/ helloworld/VSCode, output that URL using a print statement at some point in a file like views.py. The URL appears in the VS Code Terminal, where you can use Ctrl+click to open it in a browser.

When you are finished, be sure to close the browser and stop the debugger using the Stop toolbar button (the red square) or the Run ➤ Stop Debugging command (Shift+F5).

Using Definition and Peek Definition Commands

When you work with Django or any other library, you need to examine the code in those libraries from time to time. For that, VS Code provides two convenient commands that go straight to the definitions of classes and other objects in any code.

Go to Definition transfers from your code into the code that defines an object. For example, in views.py, right-click on HttpResponse in the home function and select Go to Definition (or use F12), which guides to the class definition in the Django library.

Peek Definition (or Alt+F12) is used to display the class definition directly in the editor making space in the editor window to avoid disturbing any code. To close the Peek window, press Escape or use the x in the upper right corner.

Using a Template to Render a Page

The first app created in Django usually has only plain text web pages from Python code. Even if it is possible to get HTML directly in code, developers rarely practice that because it opens the app to cross-site scripting (XSS) attacks. In the simplest hello_there function, one might think to edit the output in code with content such as = "<h1>Hello there, "+ clean_name + "!</h1>, where the result in content is attached directly to a browser. This opening lets an attacker place malicious HTML, including JavaScript code, in the URL that turns into clean_name and thus ends up being run in the browser.

Keeping HTML out of your code entirely by using templates (so that your code is concerned only with data values) is considered to be a much better practice. In Django, a template is an HTML file that accommodates placeholders for values that the code provides at run time. The Django templating engine then has to make the substitutions when rendering the page and provide automatic escaping to prevent XSS attacks. The code therefore concerns itself only with data values and markup. Django templates provide great options, such as template inheritance, which lets you define a base page with common markup and then expand upon that base by using different page-specific additions.

Begin by creating a single page using a template in the web_project/ settings.py file. First, locate the INSTALLED_APPS list and add the following entry, which makes sure the project is familiar with the app and can handle templating: 'hello'. Inside the hello folder, make a folder named templates, and then another subfolder named hello to match the app.

After that, in the templates/hello folder, create a file named hello_there.html with the following contents. This template has to have two placeholders for data values named "name" and "date", which should be separated by pairs of curly braces, {{ and }}. All other text is also considered a part of the template, together with formatting markup (such as <strong>). Template placeholders can also include formatting, such as the expressions after the pipe | symbols, in this case using Django's built-in date filter and a time filter. The code then needs only to pass the DateTime value in the following manner:[3]

```
<!DOCTYPE html>
<html>
    <head>
        <meta charset="utf-8" />
        <title>This is Django</title>
    </head>
    <body>
        <strong>Hello people, {{ name }}!</strong> It's {{ date
        | date:"l, d F, Y" }} at {{ date | time:"H:i:s" }}
    </body>
</html>
```

---

[3] Visual Studio Code, "Django Tutorial in Visual Studio Code."

At the top of views.py, add the following import statement: from Django.shortcuts import render.

Also in views.py, edit the hello_world function to use Django.shortcuts. render method for loading a template and providing the template context. The context here stands for the set of variables within the template. The render function takes the request object, followed by the path to the template relative to the templates folder, then the context object:

```python
def hello_there(request, name):

    return render(
        request,
        'helloworld/hello_world.html',
        {
            'name': name,
            'date': datetime.now()
        }
    )
```

Notice that the code looks much simpler this way, and concerned only with data values because the markup and formatting is all located in the template. Now you can start the program (inside or outside of the debugger, using Ctrl+F5), navigate to a /hello/name URL, and observe the results. You can also navigate to a /helloworld/name URL using a name like <a%20value%20that%20could%20be%20HTML> to see Django's automatic escaping in action. The "name" value in this case comes up as plain text in the browser rather than as rendering an actual element.

Serving Static Files

Static files represent content that your web app returns as-is for certain requests, such as Cascading Style Sheets files. Serving static files requires that the INSTALLED_APPS list in settings.py contains Django.contrib. staticfiles, which is included by default.

Serving static files is used when deploying to production. They work with the Django development server and also with a production server like Gunicorn. In production, you also need to set DEBUG=False in settings.py, which is necessary to carry some additional work when using containers.

Readying the App for Static Files

To get the app ready, in the project's web_project/urls.py, add the following import statement: from Django.contrib.staticfiles.URLs import staticfiles_urlpatterns. In that same file, include the following line at the end, which has standard static file URLs to the list that the project recognizes: urlpatterns += staticfiles_urlpatterns().

Referring to Static Files

To refer to static files, create a folder named static in the hello folder. Within the static folder, make a subfolder named hello, matching the app name. The reason for this extra subfolder is that when you deploy the Django project to a production server, you combine all the static files into a single folder that is served by a dedicated static file server. The static/hello subfolder makes sure that when the app's static files are combines, they are in an app-specific subfolder and will not conflict with files from other apps in the same project.

Then, in the static/hello folder, create a file named site.css with the following contents. After entering this code, also see the syntax highlighting that VS Code provides for CSS files, including a color preview:

```
.message {
    font-weight: 600;
    color: blue;
}
```

In templates/hello/hello_there.html, include the following lines after the <title> element. The {% load static %} tag is a custom Django template tag set, which lets you use {% static %} to refer to a file like the stylesheet:

```
{% load static %}
<link rel="stylesheet" type="text/css" href="{% static
'helloworld/site.css' %}" />
```

Also in templates/hello/hello_there.html, replace the contents <body> element with the following markup that uses the message style instead of a <strong> tag:

```
<span class="message">Hello, buddy {{ name }}!</span> It's
{{ date | date:'l, d F, Y' }} at {{ date | time:'H:i:s' }}.
```

Now when you run the app, navigate to a /hello/name URL and observe that the message renders in blue. Do not forget to stop the app when you are finished.

Using the Collectstatic Command

For production purposes, you would need to collect all the static files from your apps into a single folder using the python manage.py collectstatic command. You can then take a dedicated static file server to serve those files, for most issues is better overall performance. The following steps show how this collection is produced, even though you do not use the collection when running with the Django development server.

In web_project/settings.py, add the following line that identifies an exact place where static files are collected when you apply the collectstatic command:

```
STATIC_ROOT = BASE_DIR / 'static_collected'
```

Later, in the Terminal, try running the command python manage. py collectstatic and notice that hello/site.css is copied into the top-level static_collected folder altogether with manage.py. In practice, run collectstatic each time you edit static files and before forwarding it into production.

Creating Multiple Templates That Extend a Base Template

Because most web apps have multiple pages, and because those pages normally share many common items, developers split those common items into a base page template that other page templates then expand. This procedure is also called template inheritance, meaning that the extended pages inherit elements from the basic page.

Also, because you most likely need to create multiple pages that extend the same template, it is useful to create a code snippet in VS Code with which you can initialize new page templates faster. A snippet helps you prevent tedious and prone to error operations.

Creating a Base Page Template and Styles

A base page template in Django has all the shared bits of a set of pages, including references to script files. Base templates also define one or more block tags with content that extended templates are expected to override. A block tag is delineated by {% block <name> %} and {% endblock %} in both the base template and extended templates.

In the templates/hello folder, make a file named layout.html with the contents, which has blocks named "title" and "content". The markup should be able to define a simple navbar structure with links to Home, About, and Contact pages. You can use Django's {% URL %} tag to refer to other pages through the names of the corresponding URL patterns rather than by relative path. You can run the app at this point, but because you have not made use of the base template anywhere and have not changed any code files, the result will be the same.

Creating a Code Snippet

If you find yourself creating multiple pages that extend layout.html, it would save time to create a code snippet to initialize a new template file with a suitable reference to the base template. A code snippet secures a consistent part of code from a single source, which prevents mistakes that can occur when using copy-paste from active code.

To create a snippet in VS Code, select the File (Windows and Linux) or Code (macOS), menu, then follow Preferences ➤ User snippets. In the list that appears, select HTML. The option may also appear as "html.json" in the Existing Snippets section of the list if you have created snippets previously.

After VS code opens html.json, save it with Ctrl+S. Now. Any time you start typing the snippet's prefix, such as djext, VS Code will provide the snippet as an autocomplete variety. You can also use the Insert Snippet command to select a snippet from a menu.

Working with Data, Data Models, and Migrations

Many web apps operate with data stored in a database, and Django makes it pretty simple to represent the items in that database via models. In Django, a model is a Python class that comes from Django.DB.models. Model, which stands for a specific database object, most likely a table, and is located in an app's models.py file.

With Django, you administer your database through the models you define in code. Django's migrations then take care of all the details of the underlying database automatically as you modify the models over time. The general system goes the following way:

- Make changes to the models in your models.py file.

- Run python manage.py makemigrations to create scripts in the migrations folder that migrate the database from its current conditions to the new conditions.

- Run python manage.py migrate to apply the scripts to the base database.

The migration scripts can record all the incremental changes you make to your data models. By applying the migrations, Django adapts the database to match your needs. Because each incremental change has its own script, Django can automatically migrate any previous version of a database to the newly installed version. You need to occupy yourself only with your models in models.py, and not with the underlying database system or the migration scripts.

In code, you also operate only with your model classes to store and collect data, as Django handles all the other underlying details. There is only one exception that you can write data into your database, if you are using the Django administrative utility loaddata command. This command is often used to start a data set after the migrate command has been initialized.

When using the DB.sqlite3 file, you can also work directly with the database using a tool like the SQLite browser. It's fine to add or delete records in tables with it, but it is better to avoid making changes to the database schema because it will then be out of sync with your app's models. It is better to change the models, run makemigrations, and then activate migrate.

Types of Databases

By default, Django has a DB.sqlite3 file for an application database that is used for development work. SQLite works fine for low to medium traffic sites with fewer than 100 K hits per day, but is not the best option for higher volumes.[4] It is also limited to a single computer, so it cannot be applied in any multiserver scenario such as load-balancing and geo-replication. Because of this, it is best to consider using a production-level data store such as PostgreSQL, MySQL, and SQL Server. You can also apply the Azure SDK for Python to work with Azure storage services such as tables and blobs.

Migrating the Database

When you change your data models by editing models.py, you will need to update the database itself. To do so, open a Terminal in VS Code with your virtual environment activated, navigate to the project folder, and run the following commands: python manage.py makemigrations, and python manage.py migrate.

If you take a look in the migrations folder, you should now be able to see the scripts that makemigrations generates. You can also look at the database to see that the schema is updated. If you see errors when running the commands, make sure you are not using a debugging terminal that is left over from previous steps, as they may not have the virtual environment activated.

---

[4] SQLite, "When to Use SQLite," sqlite.org, accessed [date].

Creating a Superuser and Enabling the Administrative Interface

By default, Django has a great administrative interface for a web app that is protected by authentication. The interface is used through the built-in Django.contrib.admin app, which is included by default in the project's INSTALLED_APPS list (settings.py), and authentication is managed with the built-in Django.contrib.auth app, which is also built-in INSTALLED_ APPS.

You should perform the following steps to enable the administrative interface: first, create a superuser account in the app by opening a Terminal in VS Code for your virtual environment, then run the command python manage.py createsuperuser --username=<username> --email=<email>, replacing <username> and <email> using your personal information. When you run the command, Django will ask you to enter and confirm your password. Make sure you remember your username and password combination. These are the main credentials you need to authenticate with the app. Add the following URL route in the project-level urls.py (web_project/urls.py in this tutorial) to point to the built-in administrative interface:

```
path("admin/", admin.site.URLs),
```

Run the server, then open a browser to the app's /admin page (such as http://127.0.0.1:8000/admin when using the development server). Once the login page appears, enter your user credentials.

When you are fully authenticated you see the default administration page, through which you can manage users and groups. You can customize the administrative interface as you like and even provide capabilities to edit and remove entries in the database.

Flask Development

Flask is a lightweight Python framework for web applications that provides the foundation for URL routing and page rendering (Figure 4-2).

Figure 4-2. *Flask, a Python web development framework*

Flask is usually referred to as a micro framework due to the absence of features like form validation, database abstraction, and authentication. Such features are therefore provided by special Python packages called Flask extensions. These extensions seamlessly incorporate with Flask design so that they appear as if they were the segment of Flask itself. For instance, Flask does not have a page template engine, but downloading Flask includes the Jinja templating engine by default.

In this Flask section, we will review a number of features of VS Code including using the terminal, the editor, the debugger, code snippets, and others.

To start with, successfully install a version of Python 3 (options were provided earlier in this chapter). After that, you should create a virtual environment in which Flask is installed. Using a virtual environment avoids having to install Flask into a global Python environment, and gives you exact control over the libraries used in an application. A virtual environment also makes it easy to establish a requirements.txt file for the environment.

On your file system, create a project folder named hello_flask. In that folder, use the following command (depending on your computer) to create a virtual environment named env based on your current interpreter:

- **For Linux:**

  ```
  python3 -m venv env
  ```

- **For macOS:**

  ```
  python3 -m venv env
  ```

- **For Windows:**

  ```
  python -m venv env
  ```

Make sure you use a stock Python installation when activating these commands. If you use python.exe from an Anaconda installation, you will get an error because the ensurepip module is not available, and the environment is left in an unfinished state.

You can open the project folder in VS Code by running code or by running VS Code and using the File ➤ Open Folder command. In VS Code, you should open the Command Palette (View ➤ Command Palette or (Ctrl+Shift+P)). Then click on the Python: Select Interpreter command. The command will show a list of available interpreters that VS Code can provide automatically. From the list, look for the virtual environment in your project folder that starts with ./env or .\env.

Create New Integrated Terminal (Ctrl+Shift+`)) from the Command Palette, which makes up a terminal and automatically activates the virtual environment by running its activation script. However, if you are using Windows and your default terminal type is PowerShell, you might get an error that it cannot run activate.ps1 because running scripts is disabled on the system. There is no need to worry, as the error will provide a link for information on how to allow scripts. Otherwise, you can use Terminal: Select Default Shell to set "Command Prompt" or "Git Bash" as your default instead.

The selected environment should appear on the left side of the VS Code status bar, and when it does pay attention to the "(venv)" indicator that tells you that you are using a virtual environment:

- **python -m pip install --upgrade pip:** update pip in the virtual environment by running the following command in the VS Code Terminal.

- **python -m pip install flask:** install Flask in the virtual environment in the VS Code Terminal.

You now ready to write your first Flask code in a self-contained environment. VS Code activates the environment automatically when you use Terminal: Create New Integrated Terminal. When you open a separate command prompt or terminal, activate the environment by running source env/bin/activate (Linux/macOS) or env\Scripts\Activate.ps1 (Windows). You will see that the environment is activated if the command prompt shows (env) at the beginning.

Creating and Running a Minimal Flask App

In VS Code, create a new file in your project folder named app.py via File ➤ New from the menu, or by pressing Ctrl+N. After that, in app.py, add code to import Flask and create an instance of the Flask object. If you type the following code (instead of using copy-paste), you can see VS Code's IntelliSense and auto-completions:

```
from flask import Flask
app = Flask(__name__)
```

You can also insert a function or a simple string in app.py that returns content, and use Flask's app.route decorator to map the URL route / to that function:

```
@app.route("/")
def home():
    return "Hello, Flask!"
```

It is also possible to use multiple decorators on the same function, one per line, depending on how many different routes you want to map to the same function.

In the Integrated Terminal, run the app by entering python -m flask run, which then activates the Flask development server. The development server searches for app.py by default. If you run Flask, you should see output similar to the following:

```
(env) D:\py\\hello_flask_app>python -m flask run
 * Environment: production
   WARNING: Do not use the development server in a production
   environment.
   Use a production WSGI server instead.
 * Debug mode: off
 * Running on http://127.0.0.1:5000/ (Press CTRL+C to quit)
```

If you see an error, make sure you have run python -m pip install flask in your virtual environment, as described earlier. At the same time, if you want to run the development server on a different IP address or port, employ the host and port command-line arguments, as with --host=0.0.0.0 --port=80.

To open your default browser to the rendered page, Ctrl+click the http://127.0.0.1:5000/ URL in the terminal. Notice that if you visit a URL like /, a message will pop in the debug terminal showing the HTTP request: 127.0.0.1 - - [11/Jun/2021 12:40:10] "GET / HTTP/1.1" 200 -

If you want to use a different filename than app.py, such as program. py, you need to prescribe an environment variable named FLASK_APP and set its value to your open file. Flask's development server then applies the value of FLASK_APP instead of the default file app.py. When you are finished, you can stop the app by using Ctrl+C in the terminal.

Running the App in the Debugger

The Debugger tool lets you pause a running program on a particular line of code. When a program is paused you can assess variables, run code in the Debug Console panel, and otherwise take advantage of the features described on Debugging, such as automatically saving any modified files before every debugging.

Before you start you need to check that you have stopped the running app at the end of the last section by clicking Ctrl+C in the terminal. If you leave the app running in one terminal, it continues to own the port and when you run the app in the debugger using the same port, the original running app administers all the requests and you will not observe any activity in the app being debugged, and the program will not stop at breakpoints. To put it simply, if the debugger does not seem to be working, you have to make sure that no other parts of the app are still running.

Afterward, replace the contents of app.py with the following code, which adds a second route and function that you can step through in the debugger:

- from flask import Flask

- from DateTime import DateTime

- import re

```
app = Flask(__name__)

@app.route("/")
def home():
    return "Hello, Folks!"

@app.route("/helloworld/<name>")
def hello_world(name):
    now = datetime.now()
    formatted_now = now.strftime("%A, %d %B, %Y at %X")
```

When filtering the name argument to letters, use only regular expressions. URL arguments can contain arbitrary text; therefore, it is restricted to safe characters only.

The decorator applied for the new URL route, /hello/<name>, describes an endpoint /hello/ that can accept any extra value. The identifier inside < and > in the route stands for a variable that is passed to the function and can be utilized in your code.

As you already know, URL routes are case-sensitive. For instance, the route /helloworld/<name> is distinct from /HelloWorld/<name>. If you need the same function to manage both, try applying decorators for each variant. In addition, as described in the code comments, always filter arbitrary user-provided information to prevent various attacks on your app. In this case, the code filters the name argument to contain only letters, which avoids the injection of control characters and HTML. Nevertheless, when you use templates in the next project, Flask will perform automatic filtering and you will not need to script the code again.

Setting a breakpoint at the first line of code in the hello_world function (now = DateTime.now()) is quite straightforward if you do it via the following:

- Pressing F9 with the cursor on that line

- With the cursor on that line, selecting the Run Toggle Breakpoint menu command

- Clicking directly in the margin to the left of the line number

After that, you should be able to see the breakpoint appear as a red dot in the left margin.

You may switch to Run view in VS Code (using the left-side activity bar or F5), after which you may see the message "To customize Run and Debug create a launch.json file." This shows that you do not yet have a launch.json file containing various debug features. VS Code can produce those for you once you click on the create a launch.json file link.

When you select the link, VS Code will start the debug configuration. Select Flask from the dropdown and VS Code will populate a new launch. json file with a Flask run configuration. The launch.json file has a number of debugging configurations, each of which is its own JSON object within the configuration array.

Scroll down to and examine the configuration, which is named "Python: Flask". This configuration consists of "module": "flask", which tells VS Code to run Python with -m flask when it turns on the debugger. It also defines the FLASK_APP environment variable in the env property to spot the startup file, which is app.py by default but lets you easily specify a different file. When you need to change the host or port, you can use the args array. You can save launch.json simply by clicking Ctrl+S.

Next, select the Python: Flask configuration in the debug configuration list. Start the debugger by selecting the Run ➤ Start Debugging menu command, or by selecting the green Start Debugging arrow next to the list (F5). Notice how the status bar changes color to indicate debugging. A debugging toolbar also shows in VS Code containing commands in the following order: Pause (or Continue, F5), Step Over (F10), Step Into (F11), Step Out (Shift+F11), Restart (Ctrl+Shift+F5), and Stop (Shift+F5).

Output typically appears in a Python Debug Console terminal. Ctrl+click the http://127.0.0.1:5000/ link in that terminal to open a browser to that URL. In the browser's address bar, go to http://127.0.0.1:5000/ helloworld/VSCode. Before the page downloads, VS Code pauses the program at the breakpoint you establish. The small yellow arrow on the breakpoint indicates that it is the next line of code to be activated.

Use Step Over function to run the now = DateTime.now() statement. On the left side of the VS Code window, you can check out the Variables pane that shows local variables and arguments such as now and name as well as panes for Watch, Call Stack, and Breakpoints. In the Locals section, you can expand different values by double-clicking on them or using F2. Changing variables such as now, however, can break the program. Developers typically make changes only to correct values when the code did not result in the right value in the beginning.

When a program is paused, the Debug Console panel lets you try out different expressions and bits of code using the current state of the program. For instance, once you have stepped over the line now = DateTime.now(), you might test different date and time formats. For that, select the code that reads now.strftime("%A, %d %B, %Y at %X") in the editor and then right-click and select Debug: Evaluate to send that code to the debug console, where it runs:

```
now.strftime("%A, %d %B, %Y at %X")
'Sunday, 20 June, 2021 at 14:23:32'
```

The Debug Console also reveals exceptions from within the app that may not be presented in the terminal. For instance, if you see a "Paused on exception" message in the Call Stack area of Run view, switch to the Debug Console to see the exception line. After that, copy that line into the > prompt at the bottom of the debug console and try modifying the formatting:

```
now.strftime("%a, %d %B, %Y at %X")
'Sunday, 20 June, 2021 at 14:23:32'
now.strftime("%a, %d %b, %Y at %X")
'Sunday, 20 June, 2021 at 14:23:32'
now.strftime("%a, %d %b, %y at %X")
'Sunday, 20 June, 2021 at 14:23:32'
```

When you see a change you like, you can copy and paste it into the editor during a debugging session. Those changes will not be applied until you restart the debugger. You can step through a few more lines of code and then select Continue (F5) to let the program operate until the browser window shows the end result.

In order to make it easier to repeatedly navigate to a specific URL such as `http://127.0.0.1:5000/helloworld/VSCode`, output that URL using a print statement. The URL pops in the terminal where you can use Ctrl+click to open it in a browser. Be sure to close the browser and stop the debugger when you are finished by using the Stop toolbar button (the red square) or the Run ➤ Stop Debugging command (Shift+F5).

Using Definition and Peek Definition Commands

While working with Flask or any other library, you may want to review the code in those libraries themselves. VS Code has two convenient commands that operate directly to the definitions of classes and other items in any code:

- Go to Definition derives from your code into the code that describes an object. For example, in app.py, right-click on the Flask class (in the line app = Flask (__name__)) and select Go to Definition (or click F12), which goes to the class definition in the Flask library.

- Peek Definition (Alt+F12, also on the right-click context menu), is somewhat the same but shows the class definition directly in the editor (making space in the editor window without disturbing any code). To close the Peek window, press Escape to or use the x in the upper right corner.

Using a Template to Render a Page

The first app you create with Flask usually generates only plain text web pages from Python code. Although it is possible to insert HTML directly in code, developers try to avoid such a practice because it opens the app to cross-site scripting (XSS) attacks. In the hello_world function of this tutorial, for example, one might think to format the output in code with something such as content = "<h1>IIello buddy, " + clean_name + "!</h1>, where the result in content is given directly to a browser. This opening might also give some attackers a chance to place malicious HTML, including JavaScript code, in the URL that ends up in clean_name and thus ends up being run in the browser.

A much better practice is to keep HTML outside of your code completely by applying templates so that your code is concerned only with data values and not with rendering. A template is an HTML file that has placeholders for values that the code provides at run time. The templating engine mostly deals with placing the substitutions when rendering the page. The code, therefore, concerns itself only with data values, and the template concerns itself only with markup items.

The default templating engine for Flask is Jinja, which is installed at the same time as Flask. This engine provides flexible options such as automatic escaping (to avoid XSS attacks) and template inheritance. With inheritance, you can easily define a basic page with common markup and then build upon that base with page-specific additions.

In order to create a single page using a template, create a folder named templates inside the hello_flask folder, which is where Flask looks for templates by default. In that templates folder, create a file named hello_there.html with the following contents. This template requires two placeholders named "name" and "date", which are delineated by pairs of curly braces, {{ and }}.

In app.py, import Flask's render_template function near the top of the file:

```
from flask import render_template
```

Also in app.py, edit the hello_there function to use render_template to load a template and apply the named values (and include a route to recognize the case without a name). Render_template presumes that the first argument is relative to the templates folder. Normally, developers name the templates the same as the functions that use them, but matching names are not required because you always refer to the exact filename in your code:

```
@app.route("/helloworld/")
@app.route("/helloworld/<name>")
def hello_world(name = None):
    return render_template(
        "hello_world.html",
        name=name,
        date=datetime.now()
    )
```

Note that this code looks much simpler, and concerned only with data values because the markup and formatting are all fitted in the template.

After you start the program (using Ctrl+F5), navigate to a /helloworld/name URL and observe the results. You can also try navigating to a /helloworld/name URL using a name like <a%20value%20that%20could%20be%20HTML> to see Flask's automatic escaping in action. The "name" value should pop as plain text in the browser rather than as rendering an actual element.

Creating a Requirements.txt File for the Environment

When you share your app code using source control or any other method, it does not make much sense to copy all the files in a virtual environment because recipients can always refracture the environment on their own.

Therefore, developers typically skip the virtual environment folder from source control and instead write down the app's dependencies using a requirements.txt file. Even though you can create the file by hand, you can also use the pip freeze command to redesign the file based on the attached libraries in the activated environment.

Within your chosen environment, try using the Python: Select Interpreter command and run the Terminal: Create New Integrated Terminal command (Ctrl+Shift+`)) to open a terminal with that environment activated. In the same terminal, run pip freeze ➤ requirements.txt to create the requirements.txt file in your project folder.

Any recipient that gets a copy of the project needs only to run the pip install -r requirements.txt command to reload the packages with their original environment. Pip freeze has the ability to list all the Python packages you have installed in the current environment, including packages that are not currently active. The command also lists packages with precise version numbers, which you may need to convert to ranges for more applicability sometime in the future.

Lastly, bear in mind that flask-snippets is a popular VS Code extension for Flask development. However, some of snippets are often not on par with Flask development cycle, so you should exercise caution when using it.

Data Science–Specific Information and Tutorials

This section demonstrates how to use VS Code and the Microsoft Python extension with common data science libraries to recreate a basic data science scenario. Specifically, it covers how to set up a data science environment, import and clean data, create a machine learning model, and evaluate the accuracy of the generated model. Before beginning, install the Python extension for VS Code named Python and published by Microsoft from the Visual Studio Marketplace.

If you already have the full Anaconda distribution installed, then there is no need to install Miniconda. Alternatively, if you do not like using Anaconda or Miniconda, you can create a Python virtual environment and install the packages necessary for the tutorial using pip. If you opt for this route, you should at first install the following packages: pandas, jupyter, seaborn, scikit-learn, keras, and TensorFlow.

Setting Up a Data Science Environment

VS Code and the Python extension provide a great editor for data science scenarios. With native support for Jupyter Notebooks combined with Anaconda, it's easy to create an Anaconda environment with the data science modules as well as Jupyter Notebook that you will be using for creating a machine learning model.

Begin by creating an Anaconda environment for the data science tutorial by opening an Anaconda command prompt and running conda create -n myenv python=3.7 pandas jupyter seaborn scikit-learn keras TensorFlow to create an environment named myenv. Next, make a folder in the preferred location to serve as your VS Code workspace and name it hello_ds. Open the project folder in VS Code by running VS Code and using the File ➤ Open Folder command. When VS Code launches, open the Command Palette (View ➤ Command Palette or Ctrl+Shift+P) and select the Python: Select Interpreter command.

The Python: Select Interpreter command will then display a list of available interpreters that VS Code was able to indicate automatically (if you do not see the desired interpreter, see Configuring Python environments). From that list, go for the Anaconda environment you created, which should include the text 'myenv': conda.

With the environment and VS Code ready, the final step would be to create the Jupyter Notebook by opening the Command Palette (Ctrl+Shift+P) and selecting Jupyter: Create New Blank Jupyter Notebook.

As an alternative, from the VS Code File Explorer you can click on the New File icon to create a Notebook file named hello.ipynb. After that, be sure to use the Save icon on the main notebook toolbar to save the notebook with the filename hello. Once your file is created, you should try opening Jupyter Notebook in the native notebook editor.

Preparing the Data

This section shows how to load and manipulate data in your Jupyter Notebook using the Titanic dataset available on OpenML.org, which is obtained from Vanderbilt University's Department of Biostatistics at http://biostat.mc.vanderbilt.edu/DataSets. The Titanic data offers main information about the survival of passengers on the Titanic, as well as attributes about the passengers such as name and age. Using this data, you should attempt to establish a model for predicting whether a given passenger would have survived the sinking of the Titanic.

Download the Titanic data from OpenML.org as a CSV file named data. csv and save it to the hello_ds folder that you have already created in the previous section.

In VS Code, open the hello_ds folder and the Jupyter Notebook (hello.ipynb) by going to File ➤ Open Folder. Within your Jupyter Notebook, start off by importing the pandas and NumPy libraries, two libraries most used for manipulating data, and loading the Titanic data into a pandas DataFrame. Copy and paste the following code into the first cell of the notebook:

- import pandas as pd

- import numpy as np

- data = PD.read_csv('data.csv')

After that, run the cell using the Run cell icon or the Shift+Enter shortcut.

Once the cell finishes running, you can check the data that was loaded using the variable explorer and data viewer. First click on the chart icon in the notebook's upper toolbar, then the data viewer icon to the right of the data variable. You can then activate the data viewer to view, sort, and filter the rows of data. After you have analyzed the data, it can then be useful to graph some bits of it to help envision the relationships between the different variables. However, before the data can be graphed, you would need to make sure that there are not any issues with it. If you look at the Titanic CSV file, one thing you might notice is that a question mark ("?") was inserted to designate cells where data was not obtainable.

While Pandas can place this value into a DataFrame, the result for a column like Age data type will be set to Object instead of a numeric data type, which is difficult to visualize in graphs. This problem can be prevented by replacing the question mark with a missing value that pandas are able to read. To add a new cell, you can click on the insert cell icon that is in the bottom left corner of an existing cell, or use the Esc to enter command mode followed by the B key:

```
data.replace('?', np.nan, inplace= True)
data = data.astype({"age": np.float64, "fare": np.float64})
```

If you ever need to see the data type that has been utilized for a column, you can use the DataFrame dtypes attribute.

Now that the data is in good order, it is time to apply seaborn and matplotlib to see how certain columns of the dataset relate to Titanic passengers' survival chances. For that, add the following code to the next cell in your notebook and run it to see the generated plots:

- import seaborn as sns

- import matplotlib.pyplot as plt

```
fig, axs = plt.subplots(ncols=5, figsize=(30,5))
sns.violinplot(x="survived", y="age", hue="sex",
data=data, ax=axs[0])
sns.pointplot(x="sibsp", y="survived", hue="sex",
data=data, ax=axs[1])
sns.pointplot(x="parch", y="survived", hue="sex",
data=data, ax=axs[2])
sns.pointplot(x="pclass", y="survived", hue="sex",
data=data, ax=axs[3])
sns.violinplot(x="survived", y="fare", hue="sex",
data=data, ax=axs[4])
```

To better review details on the graphs, you can open them in plot viewer by sharing them over the upper left corner of the graph. These graphs are of great use when it comes to looking for some of the relationships between survival and the input variables of the data and all the possible calculate correlations between variables. To do so, all the variables used need to be numeric for the calculation and gender data stored as a string. To convert those string values to integers, script and run the following code:

```
data.replace({'male': 1, 'female': 0}, inplace=True)
```

Now that you can analyze the correlation between all the input variables, it gets simpler to identify the features that would be the best input material to a machine learning model. Statistically, the closer a value is to 1, the higher the correlation between the value and the result. You can apply the following code to correlate the relationship between all variables and survival:

```
data.corr().abs()[["survived"]]
```

Looking closely at the correlation results, you might notice that some variables, such as gender, have a fairly high correlation to survival while others, like relatives (sibsp = siblings or spouse, parch = parents or children), are likely to have little correlation.

Suppose that sibsp and parch are related in how they impact survivability potential, and group them into a new column called "relatives" to see whether the combination of them has a higher correlation level. To do this, you should check if the number of sibsp and parch is greater than 0 for a given passenger, and if so, you can then claim that they had a relative on board. Go with the following code to create a new variable and column in the dataset called relatives and check the correlation again:

```
data['relatives'] = data.apply (lambda row: int((row['sibsp'] +
row['parch']) > 0), axis=1)
data.corr().abs()[["survived"]]
```

You can also observe that when analyzed from the standpoint of whether a person had relatives, as opposed to how many relatives, there is a higher correlation with survival. With this information at disposal, you can now drop from the dataset the low-value sibsp and parch columns together with rows that had NaN values, to make a dataset that can be used for training a model.

Training and Evaluating a Model

With the dataset ready, it is time to begin creating a model. For that, it is necessary to use the scikit-learn library (as it has some of the most useful helper functions) to do processing of the dataset, train a classification model to show survivability on the Titanic, and then use that model with test data to revise its accuracy.

An ordinary first step to training a model is to split up the dataset into training and validation data. This lets you use a part of the data to train the model and another part of the data to assess the model. If you used all your data to train the model, you would not have a way to see how well it actually perform against data the model has not yet seen. An advantage of the scikit-learn library is that it comes up with a method specifically for separating a dataset into training and test data:[5]

- from sklearn.model_selection import train_test_split

  ```
  x_train, x_test, y_train, y_test = train_test_split
  (data[['sex','pclass','age','relatives','fare']],
  data.survived, test_size=0.2, random_state=0)
  ```

  Afterward, you will have to normalize the inputs in the manner that all items are treated equally. To illustrate, within the dataset, the values for an age range from ~0-100, while gender is only a 1 or 0. By normalizing all the variables, you can make sure that the ranges of values are at the same pace. Use the following code in a new code cell to scale the input values:

---

[5] Visual Studio Code, "Data Science in VS Code Tutorial," `https://code.visualstudio.com/docs/python/data-science-tutorial`, accessed July 29, 2021.

- from sklearn.preprocessing import StandardScaler

```
sc = StandardScaler()
X_train = sc.fit_transform(x_train)
X_test = sc.transform(x_test)
```

Additionally, there are a number of various machine learning algorithms that you can choose from to model the data. The scikit-learn tool provides great support for a number of them, as well as a chart to help look for the one that suits your scenario the most. As of now, you should try the Naïve Bayes algorithm, a regular algorithm for classification matters. Add a cell with the following code to create and try out the algorithm:

- from sklearn.naive_bayes import GaussianNB

```
model = GaussianNB()
model.fit(X_train, y_train)
```

With a trained model, it is possible now to try it against the test data set that was derived from training. Include and run the following code to predict the outcome of the test data and calculate the accuracy of the model:

- from sklearn import metrics

```
predict_test = model.predict(X_test)
print(metrics.accuracy_score(y_test, predict_test))
```

Judging by the result of the test data, you should have the trained algorithm resulting in ~75% success rate of estimated survival.

Utilizing Jupyter Notebooks to explore data, together with VS Code Exploring data platform, makes experimenting with ideas much easier. You can now define and run individual cells using the IPython kernel, visualize data frames, interact with plots, restart kernels, and export it all straight to Jupyter Notebooks. Moreover, when it comes to Importing Jupyter Notebooks into Python, reproducible and production-ready VS Code allows that transition to go very smoothly. With the addition of these features, you can now operate with data interactively in VS Code, making it an exciting option for those who prefer an editor for data science tasks.

Summary

In this chapter, we first started with Django development in VS Code and then moved on to Flask, familiarizing ourselves with two of the most common Python frameworks. We also talked about Data Science in relation to VS Code, and covered concepts such as Miniconda. In the next chapter we will continue with our understanding of Python coding in VS Code and unravel some new topics.

CHAPTER 5

Working with Containers and MS Azure

In the previous chapter, we learned about Django and Flask development in VS Code. In this chapter we will be talking about containers and MS Azure.

VS Code has great support for Remote Development, which is a popular feature these days. It allows you to connect to another machine via Secure Shell Protocol (SSH) and operate with code and various language services there remotely. It is also possible to connect to Microsoft Azure and manage your development environment in containers. The last two are the main focus of this chapter.

Integrating Azure for Your Python Projects

Microsoft Azure which is mostly referred to as Azure, is a cloud computing platform for building, testing, and implementing applications and services through Microsoft data management centers (Figure 5-1). It is especially important because it provides a wide array of development tools and services, such as build and production solutions.

© Sufyan bin Uzayr 2021
S. bin Uzayr, *Optimizing Visual Studio Code for Python Development*,
https://doi.org/10.1007/978-1-4842-7344-9_5

Figure 5-1. *Microsoft Azure*

It also acts as a provider of software as a service (SaaS), a platform as a service (PaaS), and infrastructure as a service (IaaS) and carries out many different programming languages, tools, and frameworks, Microsoft-based as well as third-party-specified software and systems.

In this section, we'll review some of the more import services Azure offers and then use VS Code to create a Python function that responds to HTTP requests. We'll end by deploying Docker containers to Azure App Service.

Key Azure Services

Azure utilizes large-scale virtualization at Microsoft data centers worldwide, and it supplies more than 600 services.

Computer Services

Virtual machines or infrastructure as a service (IaaS) providers allow users to create general-purpose Microsoft Windows and Linux virtual machines, as well as preconfigured machine items for in-demand software sets. Most users run Linux on Azure due to beneficial Linux distributions offered and Microsoft's own Linux-based Azure Sphere. In addition, many app services or platform as a service (PaaS) providers use Azure as an environment to let developers easily publish and administer web sites. Moreover, Azure web sites encourage developers to build sites using ASP.NET, PHP, Node.js, or Python, and deploy Team Foundation Server or uploading through the user portal. Azure customers can create web sites in PHP, ASP.NET, Node.js, or Python, or select from several open-source applications. This comprises one aspect of the platform as a service (PaaS) offerings for the Microsoft Azure Platform. Those applications that can be deployed to an App Service environment to implement background processing can be invoked on a schedule, on-demand, or run nonstop.

Identity

Popular Azure identity-focused products include:

- Azure Active Directory is used to synchronize on-premises directories and enable single sign-on.

- Azure Active Directory B2C enables access to consumer identity and access management in the cloud.

- Azure Active Directory Domain Services is activated when joining Azure virtual machines to a domain without domain controllers.

- Azure information protection is utilized to protect sensitive information.

Azure Mobile Services

- Mobile Engagement collects real-time data that highlight users' analytics. It also enables push notifications to mobile devices.

- HockeyApp can be installed to build, distribute, and run various beta tests on mobile apps.

Storage Services

Storage Services provide the audience with space for storing and accessing data on the cloud:

- Table Service lets programs store structured text in sectioned collections of items that are accessed by partition or primary keys. Azure Table Service is activated in the same manner as any other NoSQL nonrelational database.

- Blob Service offers programs a place to store unstructured text and binary data that can be accessed simply by an HTTP(S) path. Blob service also has built-in security mechanisms to limit and calculate access to data.

- Queue Service provides programs with a platform to communicate asynchronously by message using queues.

- File Service allows storing and access of data on the cloud using popular REST APIs and SMB protocols.

Data Management

- Azure Data Explorer is well-suited for big data analytics and data-exploration.

- Azure Search is great for text search and structured data filtering.

- Cosmos DB is a NoSQL database service that enacts a subset of the SQL SELECT statement on JSON documents.

- Azure Cache for Redis is a managed implementation system for Redis.

- StorSimple is great to distribute storage tasks between different devices and cloud storage.

- Azure SQL Database works to produce, scale, and place applications into the cloud using Microsoft SQL Server technology. It also integrates well with Active Directory and Microsoft System Center.

- Azure Synapse Analytics is an independently managed cloud data warehouse.

- Azure Data Factory is a data integration service that enables the creation of data-driven work processes in the cloud for automating data sets and data transformation.

- Azure Data Lake is another data storage and analytic service platform for big data analytics and massive parallel queries.

- Azure HDInsight is a data-relevant service that supports the creation of different clusters using Linux with Ubuntu.

- Azure Stream Analytics is a Serverless event processing tool that enables users to combine and run real-time analytics on multiple sets of data from sources such as devices, sensors, web sites, and even social media.

Messaging Products

The Microsoft Azure Service Bus lets applications operate on Azure premises or off-premises devices and integrate with Azure. This also allows applications to build reliable service-oriented architecture. The Azure service bus has four different types of communication mechanisms:

- Event Hubs, that provide event and telemetry functions to the cloud with low latency and high reliability. For instance, an event hub can be applied to track data from cell phones such as a GPS real-time location.

- Queues, which allow one-directional communication via service bus queue. Even though there can be multiple readers for the queue, only one can process a single message.

- Topics also provide one-directional communication but via subscriber pattern. It is similar to a queue, yet each subscriber can get a copy of the message sent to a Topic. Moreover, the subscriber can filter out messages based on various criteria set by the subscriber.

- Relays, on the other hand, provide bi-directional communication. Unlike queues and topics, a relay does not store in-flight messages in its own memory but passes data on to the destination application.

CDN

A global content delivery network (CDN) is of great use for audio, video, applications, images, and other static media files. It can be used to cache static assets of web sites geographically closer to users to advance performance. The network can be easily managed by HTTP API. As of April 2020,[1] Azure has 94 points of presence locations worldwide (also known as Edge locations).

Management

Azure Automation management tool provides a way for users to automate the manual, long-running, error-prone, and repeated tasks that are frequently performed in a cloud or virtual environment. This tool not only saves time and increases the reliability of usual administrative tasks, but also schedules them to be automatically completed at regular time periods. Moreover, you can automate processes using runbooks or automate configuration tasks using Desired State Configuration.

Azure AI

Microsoft Azure Machine Learning stands for a set of ultra-modern tools and frameworks for developers to design their own machine learning and artificial intelligence (AI) services.

Microsoft Azure Cognitive Services is another product that offers customizable services for developers to make their applications more intelligent, user-friendly, and popular. Both platforms include perceptual and cognitive intelligence covering speech recognition, speaker recognition, neural speech synthesis, face recognition, computer vision, natural language processing, and machine translation, as well as business decision services. Most AI features that are applied in Microsoft's own products and services such as Office, Teams, and Xbox are also powered by Azure Cognitive Services.

---

[1] Azure, "New Locations for Azure CDN Now Available," https://azure. microsoft.com/en-in/blog/new-locations-for-azure-cdn-now-available/, accessed July 29, 2021.

Azure Blockchain Workbench

Through Azure Blockchain Workbench, Microsoft is promoting infrastructure to set up a consortium network of multiple blockchain mechanisms. The company is also eager to provide integration from Azure Blockchain platform to other Microsoft services to share the development of distributed applications. Furthermore, Microsoft supports many general-purpose blockchains like Ethereum or Hyperledger Fabric, as well as other purpose-built blockchains like Corda.

Azure is currently available in 54 regions around the world, and is considered to be one of the first hyper-scale cloud provider that has committed to building facilities in regions located in South Africa. As of now, Azure geography has multiple Azure Regions, such as North Europe (Dublin, Ireland) and West Europe (Amsterdam, Netherlands).

Creating a Function in Azure with Python Using Visual Studio Code

In this section, we are going to use VS Code to create a Python function that responds to HTTP requests. After testing the code locally, we will try to deploy it to the serverless environment of Azure Functions.

Here are some reasons for using Python on Azure:

- You can build Python web apps in the cloud-managed application platform optimized especially for Python. It is also possible to connect your apps to data using Azure services for popular relational and nonrelational (SQL and NoSQL) databases.

- You can quickly and easily build, test, and host models from any Python environment with Azure services for data science and machine learning purposes. Azure can also bring in prebuilt AI solutions to provide the smoothest experiences to your Python apps.

- With Azure, you can build and debug your Python apps with VS Code. Moreover, Azure and VS Code also integrate seamlessly with GitHub, letting you run a full DevOps lifecycle for your Python apps.

- Azure lets you focus on your application's code, rather than on infrastructure. Meaning you can run Django and Flask apps on Azure platform with Azure Web Apps while Azure will manage the underlying app's infrastructure.

- Azure offers both relational and nonrelational databases as managed services. Most popular are MySQL, Redis, and Azure Cosmos DB (compatible with MongoDB).

Before getting started, configure your environment and make sure you have the following requirements in place: an Azure account with an active subscription and Azure Functions Core Tools version 3.x downloaded.

In order to create your local Azure Functions project in Python project using VS Code, choose the Azure icon in the Activity bar, then go to the Azure: Functions area and select the Create new project. Next, choose a directory location for your project workspace and choose Select. Be sure to sign in to Azure using your Outlook or Microsoft ID.

These simple steps were designed to be completed outside of a workspace. Therefore, you do not need to select a project folder that is already part of a workspace. Next, proceed to provide the following data at the prompts:

1. Select a language for your function project: go with Python.

2. Select a Python integration to create a virtual environment: pick a location of your Python interpreter. If the location is not displayed, script the full path to your Python binary.

3. Select a template for your project's first function: select HTTP trigger.

4. Provide a function name: type HttpExample.

5. When it comes to authorization level: opt for Anonymous, which enables everyone to call your function endpoint.

6. Set how you would like to open your project: choose to Add to the workspace.

Using this data, VS Code generates an Azure Functions project with an HTTP trigger so you can view the local project files in the Explorer.

VS Code will then integrate with Azure Functions Core tools to let you run this project on your local development computer before you publish it to Azure. To activate your function, press F5 and start the function app project. Output from Core Tools is located in the Terminal panel, and that is where your app starts. There you can also see the URL endpoint of your HTTP-triggered function operating locally.

If you have issues occurring while running on Windows, check that the default terminal for VS Code is not set to Windows Subsystem for Linux (WSL) Bash. You can also do it manually by going to the Azure: Functions area and under Functions, expand Local Project ➤ Functions. Right-click (Windows) or Ctrl-click (macOS) the HttpExample function and select Execute Function Now.

In Enter request body you should be able to see the request message body value of { "name": "Azure" }. Press Enter to send this request message to your function or manually send an HTTP GET request to the http:// localhost:7070/api/HttpExample address in a web browser. When the function is activated locally and returns a response, a notification is displayed in VS Code. Press Ctrl + C to stop Core Tools and disconnect the debugger.

After you have confirmed that the function runs properly on your local computer, you can now access VS Code to publish the project directly to Azure. However, before you can publish your app, you should sign in to Azure. If you are not already signed in, look for the Azure icon in the Activity bar, then in the Azure: Functions area, and click on Sign in to Azure. If you do not already have an Azure account, you can create a free account. If you are a student, you are eligible to create a free Azure account for Students. Once you have successfully signed in, you can close the new browser window. The subscriptions that were activated by you would be displayed in the Sidebar.

In order to publish the project to Azure, you are expected to make a function app and related resources in your Azure subscription and then deploy your code. Normally, publishing to an existing function app overwrites the content of that app in Azure. To start, choose the Azure icon in the Activity bar, then in the Azure: Functions area click on the Deploy to function app button.

You will also need to provide the following information:

1. **Select folder:** Locate a folder from your workspace or browse to one that has your function app. You will not be able to see this if you already have a valid function app running.

2. **Select subscription:** Choose the subscription to apply. You will not be able to see this if you only have one subscription.

3. **Select Function App in Azure:** Choose + Create a new Function App.

4. **Create a globally unique name for the function app:** It has to be a name that is valid in a URL path and is unique in Azure Functions at the same time.

5. **Select a runtime:** Choose the version of Python you have already activated to run locally. It is recommended to use the python --version command to check your version.

6. **Select a location for new resources:** It is always better to choose a region closer to you.

When completed, the following Azure resources are included in your subscription, using names based on your function app name:

- A resource group, which is also a logical container for related resources.

- A standard Azure Storage account, which has all the information about your projects.

- A consumption plan, which determines the host for your serverless function app.

- A function app, which defines the environment for executing your function code and lets your group functions as a logical unit for easier management and sharing of resources within the same hosting plan.

- An Application Insights are used to record the routine of your serverless function.

A notification will be displayed after your function app is created. By default, the Azure resources are set based on the function app name you provide in the same new resource group with the function app. If you need to change the names of these resources or reuse them, you would need to publish the project applying advanced create options.

Look for View Output in the notification to review the deployment results, and if you miss the notification, you can select the bell icon in the lower right corner for it to reappear again.

Back in the Azure: Functions area in the sidebar, expand your subscription, your new function app, and Functions. Right-click (Windows) or Ctrl-click (macOS) the HttpExample function and select Execute Function Now. In Enter request body you should be able to see the request message body value of { "name": "Azure" }. Press Enter to send this request message to your function so that when the function is activated in Azure and returns a response, a notification is displayed in VS Code.

Once you proceed to the next step and include an Azure Storage queue binding to your function, you will have to keep all your resources ready to be able to build over what you already have. Alternatively, you can complete the following steps to delete the function app and its related resources to avoid any additional costs:

1. In VS Code, press F1 to activate the command palette. In the command palette, look for Azure Functions: Open in the portal. Choose your function app, and press Enter to see the function app page open in the Azure portal.

2. In the Overview tab, look for the named link next to the Resource group. Choose the resource group to delete from the function app page. Proceed to the Resource group page to review the list of included resources, and click on the ones you need to delete. Keep in mind that deletion might take some

time (no more than a couple of minutes). Once
completed, a notification appears for a few seconds.
You can also click on the bell icon at the top of the
page to view the notification again.

Azure Functions lets you get access to Azure services without having
to write your own integration code. These bindings, which are represented
by input and output, are declared within the function definition. Data from
bindings are mostly presented as parameters. A trigger here is a special
type of input binding, and even if a function has only one trigger, it can
have multiple input and output bindings.

You can use VS Code to connect Azure Storage to the function. The
output binding that you insert to this function imports data from the HTTP
request to a message in an Azure Queue storage queue.

Most bindings function via stored connection strings that Functions
use to access the bound service. To put it simply, you use the Storage
account that you created with your function app. The connection to this
account is already stored in an app setting named AzureWebJobsStorage.

However, before you start to work with storage, you should install the
Azure Storage Extension for VS Code and install Azure Storage Explorer.
Storage Explorer is a great instrument to look into queue messages
produced by your output binding. Conveniently, Storage Explorer is
supported on macOS, Windows, and Linux-based operating systems. To
connect to your Storage account when running the function locally, you
should download app settings to the local.settings.json file.

Next, press the F1 key to open the command palette, then look for
and activate the command Azure Functions: Download Remote Settings.
Select Yes to all to overwrite the existing local settings. The local.settings.
json file is not published and therefore excluded from source control. Copy
the value AzureWebJobsStorage, which is the key for the Storage account
connection string value, and use this connection to confirm that the
output binding works as needed.

Because we are going to use a Queue storage output binding, you should have the Storage bindings extension downloaded before you run the project. Your project will then be configured to accommodate extension bundles, which automatically installs a predefined set of extension packages. Extension bundles usage is enabled in the host.json file at the foundation of the project, and look like this:[2]

```JSON
Copy
{
  "version": "2.0",
  "extensionBundle": {
    "id": "Microsoft.Azure.Functions.ExtensionBundle",
    "version": "[1.*, 2.0.0)"
  }
}
```

With it you can add the storage output binding to your project. Once you cover that, it is time to learn how to add an output binding. Each type of binding has a direction, type, and a unique name to be included in the function.json file. The way you define these attributes depends on the language of your function app. Binding attributes are defined directly in the function.json file and depending on the binding type, additional modifications may be needed. The queue output configuration defines the fields required for an Azure Storage queue binding.

Creating a binding is a pretty straightforward process. At first, create a binding by right-clicking (Ctrl+click on macOS) the function.json file in your HttpTrigger folder and choosing Add binding. Then follow

---

[2] Microsoft, "Quickstart: Create a Function in Azure with Python Using Visual Studio Code," https://docs.microsoft.com/en-us/azure/azure-functions/create-first-function-vs-code-python, accessed July 29, 2021.

the prompts listed in Table 5-1 to define the characteristics for the new binding.[3]

Table 5-1. *Binding characteristics*

Prompt	Value	Description
Select binding direction	Out	The binding is an output binding.
Select binding with direction...	Azure Queue Storage	The binding is an Azure Storage queue binding.
The name used to identify this binding in your code	Msg	Name that identifies the binding parameter referenced in your code.
The queue to which the message will be sent	Outqueue	The name of the queue that the binding writes to. When the *queueName* doesn't exist, the binding creates it on first use.
Select setting from "local. setting.json"	AzureWebJobsStorage	The name of an application setting that contains the connection string for the Storage account. The AzureWebJobsStorage setting contains the connection string for the Storage account you created with the function app.

---

[3] Microsoft, "Connect Azure Functions to Azure Storage Using Visual Studio Code," `https://docs.microsoft.com/en-us/azure/azure-functions/functions-add-output-binding-storage-queue-vs-code?pivots=programming-language-python`, accessed July 29, 2021.

A binding the attached to the bindings array in your function.json, which typically should look like:[4]

```
JSON
Copy
{
  "type": "queue",
  "direction": "out",
  "name": "msg",
  "queueName": "outqueue",
  "connection": "AzureWebJobsStorage"
}
```

Once the binding is defined, you can now use the name of the binding to access it as an attribute signature. With an output binding, there is no need to use the Azure Storage SDK code for authentication or queue reference, or scripting data. The Functions runtime and queue output binding will be completing these tasks for you.

In order to run the function locally, press F5 to start the function app and Core Tools. With Core Tools running, look for the Azure: Functions area. Under Functions, expand Local Project ➤ Functions then right-click (Ctrl-click on Mac) the HttpExample function and choose Execute Function Now. Once completed, you should be able to see the request message body value of { "name": "Azure" }. Press Enter to send this request message to your function, and when a response is returned, do not forget to press Ctrl + C to stop Core Tools.

Since you are using the storage connection string, your function will automatically connect to the Azure storage account when running locally. A new queue named outqueue will be made in your storage account by the

---

[4] Microsoft, "Connect Azure Functions to Azure Storage Using Visual Studio Code."

Functions runtime when the output binding is first activated. The Storage Explorer will then be used to demonstrate that the queue was created along with the new message.

In order to connect Storage Explorer to your account, it is necessary to run the Azure Storage Explorer tool. Select the connect icon on the left, and click on Add an account. In the Connect dialog, choose Add an Azure account, choose your Azure environment, and select Sign in. After you successfully sign in to your account, you will be able to see all of the Azure subscriptions attached to your account.

To examine the output queue in VS Code, press the F1 key to open the command palette, then search for and run the command Azure Storage: Open in Storage Explorer and look for your Storage account name. Your storage account opens in Azure Storage Explorer.

You should then expand the Queues node and select the queue named outqueue. The queue carries the message that the queue output binding created when you ran the HTTP-triggered function. If you activated the function with the default name value of Azure, the queue message is Name passed to the function: Azure. Try running the function again, send another request, and you will be able to see a new message appear in the queue. With it, it is now time to redeploy and verify the updated app.

Go to VS Code, press F1 to open the command palette in which you should search for, and select Azure Functions: Deploy to function app. Choose the function app that you created in the first article and deploy it to dismiss the warning about overwriting files.

Once the deployment completes, you can again employ the Execute Function Now feature to trigger the function in Azure and view the message in the storage queue to verify that the output binding creates a new message in the queue.

In Azure, resources refer to function apps, functions, and storage accounts. They are grouped into resource groups, and you can remove everything in a group simply by deleting the whole group.

Press F1 in VS Code to open the command palette. In the command palette, look for and select Azure Functions: Open in the portal. Choose your function app and press Enter. The function app page will then open in the Azure portal. In the Overview tab, select the named link next to the Resource group. Here, select the resource group to delete from the function app page and verify that they are the ones you want to delete. Select Delete resource group, and simply follow the instructions. Deletion may take a couple of minutes, and when it is completed, a notification will show up for just a few seconds.

In the next section, we will discuss how to deploy Docker containers to App Services in Azure.

Deploying Docker Containers to Azure App Service

Once you have installed the Azure extension, go to the Azure explorer and select Sign in to Azure to follow with the prompts. After signing in, confirm that Azure: Signed In statement appears in the Status Bar and your subscription is displayed in the Azure explorer as well.

If you see the "Cannot find subscription with that name," the error might be due to the fact that you are behind a proxy and cannot reach the Azure API. You can easily configure HTTP_PROXY and HTTPS_PROXY environment variables with your proxy information in your terminal:[5]

- **For Windows:**

```
set HTTPS_PROXY=https://username:password@proxy:8080
set HTTP_PROXY=http://username:password@proxy:8080
```

---

[5] Microsoft, "Tutorial: Deploy Docker Containers to Azure App Service with Visual Studio Code," `https://docs.microsoft.com/en-us/azure/developer/python/tutorial-deploy-containers-01`, accessed July 29, 2021.

- **For macOS and Linux:**

```
export HTTPS_PROXY=https://username:password@proxy:8080
export HTTP_PROXY=http://username:password@proxy:8080
```

With a container image in a registry, you can apply the Docker
extension in VS Code to set up an Azure App Service operating the
container. In the Docker explorer, expand Registries, expand the node for
your registry, then expand the node for your image name until you see the
image with the :latest tag.

You can locate an image in the Docker explorer by right-clicking the
image and selecting Deploy Image to Azure App Service. Select the Deploy
Image to Azure App Service menu item. Afterward, follow the prompts to
select an Azure subscription, select or specify a resource group, specify a
region, configure an App Service Plan, and set a name for the site.

The name of the App Service should be unique across all of Azure, so it
is standard to use a company or personal name. For production sites, you
can configure the App Service with a separately registered domain name.
Setting the app service as such takes not more than just a few minutes, and
you can see progress in VS Code's Output panel.

Once over, you should also add a setting named WEBSITES_PORT
to the App Service to specify the port on which the container is located.
It is typical to use an image from the Create a Python container in VS
Code tutorial with the port of 5000 for Flask and 8000 for Django. To set
WEBSITES_PORT of your own, switch to the Azure: App Service explorer,
expand the node for your new App Service, and right-click Application
Settings to select Add New Setting. In the beginning, be sure to enter
WEBSITES_PORT as the key and the port number as the value.

The App Service restarts automatically when you change settings. You
can also right-click the App Service and select Restart at any time. After the
service has restarted, browse the site at HTTP://<name>.azurewebsites.

net. You can use Ctrl+ click (Cmd + click on macOS) on the URL in the Output panel, or right-click the App Service in the Azure: App Service explorer and select Browse Website.

Because you are going to make changes to your app at some point for sure, you end up rebuilding your container many times. Fortunately, the process consists of only a few steps. First, rebuild the Docker image. If you change only the app code, the build should take only a few seconds. Then, push your image to the registry. Similarly, if you modify only the but app code, only that small layer needs to be pushed, and the process will be completed within seconds.

After that, in the Azure: App Service explorer, right-click the suitable App Service and select Restart. Restarting an app service will automatically deliver the latest container image from the registry. After about 15–20 seconds, try visiting the App Service URL again to check the updates.

You can also use this procedure to stream logs from an Azure App Service for a container to VS Code. From within VS Code, you can view logs from the running site on Azure App Service, that detains any output to the console and directs them to the VS Code Output panel. In order to open VS Code Output panel with a connection to the log stream, find the app in the Azure: App Service explorer, right-click the app, and choose Start Streaming Logs. Be sure to answer Yes when asked to enable logging and restart the app.

It is possible that Azure resources you established for your project might incur ongoing costs. To prevent overspending, delete the resource group that hosts all those resources. You can delete the resource group through the Azure portal or the Azure CLI: In the Azure portal. Select Resource groups from the left-side navigation pane, select the resource group that you want to be erased, and then use the Delete function.

Then run the following Azure CLI command , but replace <resource_group> with the name of the selected group:

```
az group delete --no-wait --name <resource_group>
```

Following are some of the most popular Azure extensions for VS Code that you may find useful for this operation:

- Cosmos DB

- Azure Functions

- Azure CLI Tools

- Azure Resource Manager Tools

Using Containers in VS Code

The VS Code Remote Containers extension enables you to use a Docker container as a full-featured virtual environment. It lets you access any folder inside a container and take advantage of VS Code's attribute set. A devcontainer.json file in your project is there to guide VS Code on the creation of a development container with a well-defined runtime set (Figure 5-2). This container can be utilized to operate an application or to disconnect tools, libraries, or runtimes that are necessary for dealing with a codebase.

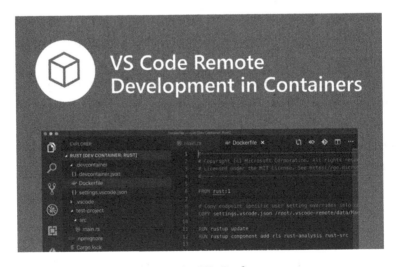

Figure 5-2. Remote containers in VS Code

Workspace files are installed from the local file system or shared or copied into the container. Extensions are activated inside the container, where they have full access to the tools, platform, and another file system. This gives you a chance to seamlessly switch your entire development environment by linking to a different container. This lets VS Code run a smooth local-quality development experience—including full IntelliSense capacity, code navigation, and debugging—regardless of where your code is located.

There are a few system requirements that come with installing containers in VS Code:

- **Windows:** You are expected to have Docker Desktop 2.0+ on Windows 10 Pro/Enterprise. Windows 10 Home (2004+) requires Docker Desktop 2.3+ and the WSL 2 back-end.

- **macOS:** Be sure to set Docker Desktop 2.0+.

- **Linux:** Docker CE/EE 18.06+ and Docker Compose 1.21+.

To get started, first install and configure Docker for your operating system. If you are using WSL 2 on Windows, to enable the Windows WSL 2 back-end: Right-click on the Docker taskbar item and select Settings. Check Use the WSL 2 based engine and verify your distribution is enabled under Resources ➤ WSL Integration. Then right-click on the Docker taskbar item, select Settings, and update Resources ➤ File Sharing with any locations your source code is located.

If you are using Linux, follow the official install instructions for Docker CE/EE for your distribution and add your user to the docker group by using a terminal to run: sudo usermod -aG docker $USER. Then sign out and back in again to set your changes before you install the VS Code and Remote Development extension pack.

If you are working with Git, there are two points to consider: if you are working with the same repository both locally in Windows and inside a container, see that you set up stable line endings. If you copy using a Git credential manager, it is important that your container has a full access to your credentials.

Operating with Containers

The Remote containers extension administers in two primary operating models: you can use a container as your full-time development environment, or attach it to another running container to examine it. The easiest way to get started is to try one of the sample development containers from the Docker and the Remote-Containers extension where you can select a sample from the extensive list.

On the other hand, you can open an existing folder in a container for any project to use as your full-time development environment by applying active source code on your filesystem. Start VS Code, run the Remote-Containers: Open Folder in Container command from the Command Palette (F1), and click on the project folder for which you need to set up the container. At the same time, if you want to modify the container's contents or settings before opening the folder, you can activate Remote-Containers: Add Development Container Configuration Files instead. Next, pick a starting point for your dev container. You can opt for a base dev container definition from a filterable list, or use an existing Dockerfile or Docker Compose file. Please pay attention when using Alpine Linux containers, as some extensions may not be available due to glibc dependencies in native code inside the extension.

The filterable list will be automatically organized based on the contents of the folder you have. The dev container definitions typically come from the vscode-dev-containers repository. You can easily look through the containers folder of that repository to check the contents of each definition. After selecting the starting point for your container, VS

Code will include the dev container configuration files in your project (.devcontainer/devcontainer.JSON).

The VS Code window will then restart and build the dev container. You only have to build a dev container the first time you access it; opening the folder after the first successful build will be much faster. A progress notification will be there to display status updates. After the build is over, VS Code will automatically connect to the container. You can then interact with your project in VS Code just as you could when accessing the project locally: when you open the project folder, VS Code will pick up and reuse your dev container configuration by default. While using this approach to link-local filesystem into a container is convenient, it does have some minor performance overhead on Windows and macOS.

If you are using Windows Subsystem for Linux v2 (WSL 2) and have activated Docker Desktop's WSL 2 back-end, you can work with source code stored inside WSL.

Once the WSL 2 engine is enabled, you can either use the Remote-Containers: Reopen Folder in Container command from a folder that is already opened or select Remote-Containers: Open Folder in Container from the Command Palette (F1) and choose a WSL folder using the local \\wsl$ share (from the Windows side).

You can also open an existing workspace in a container following a similar process to open a VS Code multiroot workspace in a single container if the workspace only references relative paths to subfolders. In this case, you can apply the Remote-Containers: Open Workspace in Container command or simply use File ➤ Open Workspace once you have opened a folder that contains a .code-workspace file in a container. Once connected, you should add the .devcontainer folder to the workspace so you can edit its contents with ease, if it is not already visible. Remember that while it is not possible to use multiple containers for the same workspace in the same VS Code window, it is possible to use multiple Docker Compose operated containers at once from separate windows.

Creating a Devcontainer.json File

VS Code's container configuration is located in a devcontainer.json file. This file is optional, but it is recommended that you create it because it makes handling debugging configuration easier.

This file is the same as the launch.json file for debugging configurations, but is mostly applied for launching (or adding to) your development container. You can also determine which extension to install once the container is running or postconstruct commands to arrange the environment. The dev container configuration is either located under .devcontainer/devcontainer.JSON or stored as a .devcontainer.JSON file in the foundation of your project. You can use any image, Dockerfile, or set of Docker Compose files with it as a starting point. Here is an ordinary example that includes one of the prebuilt VS Code Development Container images:[6]

```
{
    "image": "mcr.microsoft.com/vscode/devcontainers/
    typescript-node:0-12",
    "forwardPorts": [3000],
    "extensions": ["dbaeumer.vscode-eslint"]
}
```

Activating the Remote-Containers: Add Development Container Configuration Files command from the Command Palette (F1) will deliver the needed files to your project as a starting point, which you can further edit to match your needs. The command also allows you to pick a prescribed container configuration from a list based on your folder's contents, reuse an existing Dockerfile, or reuse an existing Docker Compose file.

---

[6] Microsoft, "Redeploy a Container to Azure App Service After Making Changes," https://docs.microsoft.com/en-us/azure/developer/python/ tutorial-deploy-containers-03, accessed July 29, 2021.

At times you might have an occasion where you are using a Docker named volume that you need to review or make changes in. You can activate VS Code to work with these contents without creating or editing devcontainer.json file but by selecting the Remote-Containers: Explore a Volume in a Development Container from the Command Palette (F1).

In addition, it is also possible to inspect your volumes in the Remote Explorer. First, select Containers in the dropdown, where you can find a Dev Volumes section. Right-click on a volume to check its creation information, such as when the volume was made and what files were cloned into it. If you have the Docker extension installed, you can right-click on a volume in the Volumes section of the Docker Explorer and select Explore in a Development Container to explore and navigate through the whole Docker context menu.

Managing Extensions

VS Code manages and stores extensions in one of two places: locally on the UI/client side, or in the container. While extensions that directly impact the VS Code UI, such as themes and snippets, are uploaded locally, most extensions will be placed inside a particular container. This feature lets you install only the extensions you need for a specific task in a container and effortlessly turn the whole tool-chain on by linking to a new container.

When you install an extension from the Extensions view, it will automatically be placed in the correct location. You can guess where an extension is installed by looking at the category grouping. There will be a Local - Installed category and also one for your container. Local extensions that actually need to operate remotely will appear Disabled in the Local - Installed category. In order to install an extension on your remote host, select Install. You can also install all locally installed extensions inside the Dev Container by accessing the Extensions view and clicking Install Local Extensions in Dev Container: [Name], pressing the cloud button at the right of the Local - Installed title bar. This will present a dropdown from which you can choose what locally installed extensions to add to your container.

Some extensions may depend upon you installing additional software in the container. Even though you can edit your devcontainer.json file by hand to add a list of extension IDs, you can also right-click on any extension in the Extensions view and click Add to devcontainer.json.

If there are some extensions that you would need to have installed in any container, you should update the remote.containers.defaultExtensions User setting. To illustrate, if you wanted to install the GitLens and Resource Monitor extensions, you would have to script their extension IDs in the following manner:[7]

```
"remote.containers.defaultExtensions": [
    "eamodio.gitlens",
    "mutantdino.resourcemonitor"
]
```

Forcing an Extension to Operate Locally or Remotely

Extensions are usually produced and tested to either operate locally or remotely, but not both. Nevertheless, if an extension supports it, it is possible to modify it to run in a particular location in your settings.json file. For instance, the following setting will make the Docker extension run locally and Debugger for Chrome extension run remotely, despite their default settings:[8]

```
"remote.extensionKind": {
    "ms-azuretools.vscode-docker": [ "ui" ],
    "msjsdiag.debugger-for-chrome": [ "workspace" ]
}
```

---

[7] Microsoft, "Redeploy a Container to Azure App Service After Making Changes."

[8] Microsoft, "Redeploy a Container to Azure App Service After Making Changes."

A value of "ui" instead of "workspace" is the one that will force the extension to operate on the local UI/client-side instead. Normally, this should only be applied for testing unless otherwise guided by the extension's documentation, since it can cause errors in extensions.

Forwarding or Publishing a Port

Containers are naturally unrelated environments, so if you need to access a server, service, or another source inside your container, you will have to forward or publish the port to your host. You can potentially configure your container to always keep these ports open, or forward them for the time being.

You can also settle a list of ports you want to forward at all times when attaching or accessing a folder in a container by using the forwardPorts function in devcontainer.json, similar to "forwardPorts": [3000, 3001]. After that, you are requested to reload and reopen the window for all the settings to be applied once VS Code connects to the container again.

Temporarily Forwarding a Port

If you need to access a port that was not included in devcontainer.json, or if you need to publish it in your Docker Compose file, you can forward a new port for the duration of the session by activating the Forward a Port command from the Command Palette (F1). After choosing a port, a notification will inform you about the localhost port you should use to access the port in the container. For example, when you forward an HTTP server listening on port 3000, the notification will tell you that it is mapped to port 3000 on localhost. You can then create a link to this remote HTTP server using http://localhost:3000.

If you would like VS Code to recollect any ports you have previously forwarded, check Remote: Restore Forwarded Ports in the Settings editor (Ctrl+,) or set "remote.restoreForwardedPorts": true in settings.json.

Docker also has the ability to publish ports when the container is created. Published ports have very much the same pattern as ports that you make available to your local network. If your application only accepts calls from localhost, it will dismiss connections from published ports just as your local machine would for network calls. Forwarded ports, on the other hand, actually look like localhost to the application. Each can be beneficial in different instances.

To publish a port, you can utilize the appPort item. For example, when you reference an image or Dockerfile in devcontainer.json, you can use the appPort property to publish ports to the host: "appPort": [3000, "8921:5000"].

Similarly, you can access the Docker Compose ports mapping that can easily be attached to your docker-compose.yml file to publish additional ports:

```
- "3000"
- "8921:5000"
```

In any case, you would have to rebuild your container for the setting to have any impact. You can achieve this by starting off the Remote-Containers: Rebuild Container command in the Command Palette (F1) when you are linked to the container.

Opening a terminal in a container from VS Code is also quite simple. When you create a folder in a container, any terminal window you open in VS Code (via Terminal ➤ New Terminal) will automatically operate in the container rather than locally. You can also use the same code command line from this same terminal window to take a number of different operations, such as opening a new file or folder in the container.

Once you have opened a folder in a container, you can switch the VS Code's debugger on in the same way you would when performing the application locally. For instance, if you choose to launch configuration in launch.json and start debugging (F5), the application will turn on the remote host and add the debugger to it.

VS Code's local user settings are also reapplied when you are linked to a dev container. Even though this keeps your user experience stable, you might want to vary some of these settings between your local project and the container. When you have connected to a container, you can also calibrate container-specific settings by running the Preferences: Open Remote Settings command from the Command Palette (F1) or by switching to the Remote tab in the Settings editor. These will overrule any local settings you currently activate every time you connect to the container.

By default, the Remote-Containers extension automatically kicks off the containers attached to the devcontainer.json when you open the folder. When you close VS Code, the extension automatically turns off the containers you have connected to. However, you can correct this behavior by adding "shutdownAction": "none" to devcontainer.json.

While you can utilize the command line to administer over your containers, you can also do it with the Remote Explorer. To stop a container, choose Containers from the dropdown list and right-click on a running container, then select Stop Container. You can also kick off exited containers, remove containers, and remove recent folders. Through the Details view, you can forward ports and open already forwarded items in the browser. When you need to clean out images or mass-delete containers, look for Cleaning out unused containers and images for various available options.

Personalizing with Dotfile Repositories

Dotfiles stand for files whose filename starts with a dot (.) and generally have configuration information for different applications. Because development containers can make up for a wide range of application types, it could be convenient to place these files somewhere so that you can easily duplicate them into a container once it is on and operating. A practical way to do this would be to locate these dotfiles in a GitHub repository and then apply a utility to take a copy and employ them. The Remote-Containers extension has built-in assistance for using these with your own containers. If you are a newbie in this area, start by taking a look at the different dotfiles bootstrap repositories that are available.

At the same time, there are known limitations to remote containers:

- Docker Toolbox on Windows is not supported.

- Windows container images are not yet supported.

- Using a remote Docker Host is realizable, but requires extra setup actions.

- All roots and folders in a multiroot workspace will be accessed in the same container, regardless of whether there are available configuration documents at lower levels or not.

- The unofficial Ubuntu Docker snap set for Linux is not supported.

- If you copy a Git repository with SSH and your SSH key has a passcode, VS Code's pull and sync features may break off when running remotely. Either use an SSH key without a passphrase, copy using HTTPS, or run git push from the command line to operate around the matter.

- Local proxy settings are not reapplied inside the container, which can obstruct extensions from working unless the correct proxy data is configured (for example, global HTTP_PROXY or HTTPS_PROXY environment items with the accurate proxy data).

Additionally, the first-time installation of Docker Desktop for Windows without the WSL 2 engine might require an additional sharing action to provide your container with access to local source code. This step may not work with certain email-based identities, and you may get errors if you sign in to Docker with your email address instead of your Docker ID. This is a known problem and can be resolved by signing in with your Docker ID instead.

Summary

In this chapter we unraveled the mighty world of MS Azure services, and how it can be used for building and deploying terrific Python apps.

Index

A

Azure Blockchain Workbench, 174

Azure services

AI, 173

binding, 182

CDN, 172

CLI command, 187

computer, 168, 169

data management, 170, 171

deploy Docker, 185–187

Docker, 185

functions, 177, 179, 180

identity, 169

management, 173

message, 172

mobile, 169

storage, 170

VS Code, 174–177

Azure Storage queue binding, 179, 181, 182

B

Better Comments extension, 62

Breakpoints, 90

app types, 90

invoke, 90

validation, 90

C

Command Palette, 10, 11, 13, 74–77, 84, 95, 96, 98, 107, 108, 118, 148, 160

Conda environment, 94, 95, 160

Config files, 118

JUPYTER_CONFIG_DIR, 119

JUPYTER_CONFIG_PATH, 119

Content delivery network (CDN), 172

Cross-site request forgery (CSRF), 125

Cross-site Scripting (XSS), 125, 137

customTemplatePath configuration, 65

D, E

Data files, 120

JUPYTER_DATA_DIR, 121

JUPYTER_PATH, 120

Data science

preparing data, 160–163

setting up environment, 159

training/evaluating model, 164, 165

Data viewer, 115, 161

© Sufyan bin Uzayr 2021
S. bin Uzayr, *Optimizing Visual Studio Code for Python Development*,
https://doi.org/10.1007/978-1-4842-7344-9

W, X, Y, Z

Printed in the United States
by Baker & Taylor Publisher Services